Worrying

Francis O'Gorman has written widely on English literature chiefly from 1780 to the present, and mostly, but not exclusively, on poetry and nonfictional prose. His recent publications include editions of John Ruskin's *Praeterita* (Oxford World's Classics, 2012), Elizabeth Gaskell's *Sylvia's Lovers* (Oxford World's Classics, 2014), and a co-edited edition, with Katherine Mullin, of Anthony Trollope's *Framley Parsonage* (Oxford World's Classics, 2014). He edited *The Cambridge Companion to John Ruskin* (Cambridge University Press, 2015). Recent essays have been on Philip Larkin, Wordsworth, Swinburne, James Joyce, T. S. Eliot, Gerard Manley Hopkins, Tennyson, and the state of the modern English university. Francis O'Gorman—from English, Irish, and Hungarian families—was educated at the University of Oxford and is currently a Professor in the School of English at the University of Leeds. He spends his spare time playing music, walking in the Yorkshire Dales, traveling around Europe, and sitting in bars.

Worrying

A Literary and Cultural History

Francis O'Gorman

Bloomsbury Academic
An imprint of Bloomsbury Publishing Inc

B L O O M S B U R Y
NEW YORK · LONDON · OXFORD · NEW DELHI · SYDNEY

Bloomsbury Academic
An imprint of Bloomsbury Publishing Inc

1385 Broadway	50 Bedford Square
New York	London
NY 10018	WC1B 3DP
USA	UK

www.bloomsbury.com

BLOOMSBURY and the Diana logo are trademarks of Bloomsbury Publishing Plc

First published 2015
Reprinted by Bloomsbury Academic 2015 (four times)

© Francis O'Gorman, 2015

Library of Congress Cataloging-in-Publication Data
O'Gorman, Francis.
Worrying : a literary and cultural history / Francis O'Gorman.
pages cm
Summary: "A literary and cultural exploration of worry and the modern mind" – Provided by publisher.
Includes bibliographical references and index.
ISBN 978-1-4411-5129-2 (hardback) – ISBN 978-1-4411-8128-2 (ePub) – ISBN 978-1-4411-4360-0 (ePDF) 1. Worry. 2. Uncertainty. 3. Worry in literature. I. Title.
BF575.W8.O46 2015
152.4'609–dc23
2014045774

ISBN: HB: 978-1-4411-5129-2
ePub: 978-1-4411-8128-2
ePDF: 978-1-4411-4360-0

Typeset by Newgen Knowledge Works (P) Ltd., Chennai, India
Printed and bound in the United States of America

"What if . . . ?"

Contents

Preface

*Cetera per terras omnis animalia somno
laxabant curas et corda oblita laborum*

P. VERGILIUS MARO, *Aeneid*, IX.224–5

*(All other living creatures on earth were asleep, their worries
Dissolved in sleep, their minds oblivious of toil and trouble)*[1]

It's 4.06 a.m.

There's no light in the bedroom—and almost no sound. The street outside is absolutely empty. There's the quietest breathing inside: of my partner; of three cats. They're all fast asleep.

There's no disturbance in the air, nothing but almost-darkness, almost-stillness, and the closest a city-center house can come to dead silence in the dead of night.

But within my head there's a noise. There are all the sounds of fretful attention. There is the opposite of the environment: churning, repeating, pounding noise.

I'm wide awake—the kind of awakeness that is only possible in the middle of night, when nothing is quite in proportion, when what is on my mind feels luminously real, troubling, and urgent.

But I'm not sick. I am not hallucinating. I have no mental condition that would even vaguely interest a doctor. At one level, I am absolutely

---

[1]Virgil, *The Aeneid*, trans. Cecil Day-Lewis (Oxford: Oxford University Press, 1986), p. 257.

fine. Much of the security of my life is all around me. Much that I care about is lying literally next to me, safe and well. Those that I love, here and away, are fine.

So what on earth is the matter? What *is* all this noise?

The answer is neither glamorous nor, on the surface, very interesting. But it is at least true.

I am worried.

I'm fretting about a difficult meeting with an exceptionally troublesome person later in the morning. The nineteenth-century English novelist Anthony Trollope said in *Orley Farm* (1861–2) that "There is nothing perhaps so generally consoling to a man as a well-established grievance; a feeling of having been injured, on which his mind can brood."[2] That's meant to be funny. But right now, I can't see it.

I'm running through what seem to me my grievances, shifting between anger and trepidation, wondering what will be the outcome of our encounter. I need to keep my cool. I must not capitulate. I am just as good as he is. If not better. Yes! Better. He mustn't get the upper hand. I must not let him get away with such contemptuous behavior. I must let him know that this isn't acceptable but politely, in a measured way.

I've been worrying about this for some time. In fact, I've just returned from a short break in Venice. Venice is my favorite city. But this trip to the city of the Most Serene was bothersome, half-shadowed by my worries. I could barely focus long on Venice's charms. I looked through the *palazzi* and the *campi* to the source of my trouble. Worry ate into my day. It poisoned the *prosecco*, soured the *sarde in saor*. I fretted about the outcome of the meeting. The encounter cast its shadow long and far, like that of the San Marco *campanile*. The future

[2]Anthony Trollope, *Orley Farm*, 2 vols (London: Chapman and Hall, 1862), i.64.

beyond the meeting seemed uncertain and I tormented myself with all sorts of unlikely consequences. Was I right to berate him? Would he pull some rhetorical rabbit out of the hat and prove me wrong, even though, in truth, *he* was? Why would he not understand that he was *unpleasant*?

It was the anticipation of conflict, of meeting contempt, of encountering aloof disdain that was upsetting. There was a forthcoming quarrel, for sure.

But what it would lead to, I didn't know.

I could, however, imagine. And in the early hours of the morning, worried imaginations lose hold on sensible things.

I couldn't get either the meeting or the individual out of my mind either in Venice or now, however much I told myself that neither he nor the meeting was worth it.

No! He was not worth it.

4.32 a.m. . . . still worrying . . .

This is a book about that sort of experience, in all its many forms, and arising from many occasions. I call them "worries" though, as I go on to show, what is really important about them is not the name but the extraordinary multiplicity and contemporaneity of their nature. Worries, to say the least, are protean. They appear in a range of different shapes. They take over many minds. They are, of nature, like a strangling weed: they can't be eradicated even if they can be cut back. They keep growing. They smother. They are exceptionally good at spoiling the view. And they are part of now.

This is a book about the business of worrying and about the business of a *man* worrying when worry has often been thought a woman's terrain. Certainly, it is neither sex nor gender that defines the borderlands of worrying in this book. And if the recurrent experience of fretting over an unknown future means nothing to you, please stop reading now. If the question *"what if . . .?"* is a stranger, please don't read further. You are safe. You are, in a sense, blessed. You are an object of envy. Certainly, you're not one of us. My book is for those who, instinctively and intimately, know what I am talking about. We live with worry. If you know what I am talking about, please carry on reading.

This book is for you.

Worrying takes being worried, as I will try to define it, seriously. It uncovers the significance of worrying for who we are. It reads meaning into worrying. It does so in a way that is without obvious parallel and without a method that's well-tried. This is not a medical book or, certainly not, a self-help book. It's not an autobiography though there is plenty about me in it. *Worrying* is not really a history or a volume about literary representations, despite my subtitle, though there is something of both those to come. This study is, rather, a literary and philosophical meditation on the meaning of worry, where it comes from, and how it came to be our companion. *Worrying* historicizes though is not quite history and it philosophizes though it is not quite philosophy. It's a book that takes its approach from its subject. *Worrying* worries at worry.

The first chapter pins down a working definition of worry—it'll have to do—as a set of anxieties about an unknown future usually predicated on "*what if . . .?*" questions. I think about the relationship between words and worry, and discuss why worry is, or at least has been, difficult to discuss. I come face to face with the embarrassment of worrying and of being a worrier. The chapter also provides a "short history" of worry by examining the arrival of the concept as we recognize it now in the nineteenth century and its emergence in the early twentieth century as a familiar but also awkward category of experience. The chapter considers both the burgeoning of self-help books in the years around the First World War and the literary manifestations of a critical awareness of worry as a label for a human experience, including an account of writers who either represent worry as a significant state of mind or who encourage a form of "worried reading" of their work. The chapter also continues the discussion of the invisibility of worry and its association with particular kinds of people, with a particular definition of modern individuality.

The second chapter muses on the established strategies, from the beginning of the twentieth century onward, to "deal" with worry. Considering the range of self-help books, I think about their methods and their strong sense that beliefs about the self are at the roots of worry. This prompts me to reflect on what changes us, on how we respond to and incorporate new ideas or perspectives on our own lives, and how difficult it is to hold on to a new belief about ourselves if, at the bottom, we don't believe it. Belief emerges in the chapter as a central problem of worry; a practice of mind that reveals to us just how much of our apparently rational life is founded in a priori faith on the back of which we build arguments and justifications—and worries. The chapter includes some reflection on the ways in which we worriers use nonrational or beyond-rational techniques for dealing with worries, opening the lid on the strange world of charms and rites that even the most well-educated and sensible people secretly deploy to placate the revenging powers that, at some level, are present in the worrier's mind. This portion of the chapter presents worrying as an odd form of revenge tragedy.

Where belief as a ground of worry is the subject of Chapter 2, the subject of Chapter 3 is worry's emergence from reason. The macro-history of worrying involves recognition that worrying is, for a start, something like a form of reason—an attempt to enumerate and evaluate different possibilities for the future with the aid of logical analysis that seeks to take everything into account. Worrying *seems* like a rational activity even if it usually fails to decide the most likely outcome, preferring instead to concentrate on the least welcome outcome or simply on possibilities. Yet worry's relationship with reason is more than this because worry is only possible in a world of choice. My chapter looks at the whole cultural myth of the "birth of reason," of the fantasized change from faith to thought as the guiding power of human lives. With an affirmation of the importance and possibility of human choice, and on reasoning as a way of deciding the best options, the mythic shift from faith to reason is the portal through which the insomniac, drained shape of worry has slipped. The chapter considers some literary and visual representations of thinking, reflecting on how difficult it is to *imagine* a world of faith, and, in visual arts, how difficult it is to distinguish the modern act of thinking from the experience of fretting.

The rest of the third chapter considers contemporary matters arising from this macro-history. I think about a succession of philosophical and political ideas that seem to me to be betrayed by worry or for which worry provides the basis for a critique. Much of the focus of this book is lightly philosophical. Many of its terms have long histories in philosophical debate: the future, plausibility, causal relations, reasonableness, language's relation to the mind. But it is explicitly to philosophers I turn when thinking about the directions in which reason can take us. First, I think about the liberal ambitions of the Victorian intellectual John Stuart Mill (1806–73) to reach decision through free and reasoned thought and to increase human well-being by doing so. The chapter adopts the worrier's understanding of reason as unable to reach secure conclusions so that, in turn, it offers a critical commentary on Mill's assumptions. Similarly, I take the worrier's realization that reason doesn't lead to conclusions conducive to the extension of well-being as another factor missing from Mill's optimism. A sense of the worrier's understanding of unhappiness as *valuable*, which emerges from this section, is picked up in the final chapter. Second, I look at the operation of powerful political ideas in the modern world. I consider particularly the notion of choice in a free market; the conception of a "free" human being; and the conviction that social harmony and the optimal conditions for living will be achieved by the "liberation" of all men and women freely to pursue their own desires and "destinies." I admit the element of the quixotic about my method but I nevertheless propose that the experience of worrying about choice, and of how human "liberty" might be understood by a worrier, is a cryptic form of political philosophy quite at odds with the direction of advanced capitalism in the West.

The final chapter is a looser structure. It takes on, at first, the unlikely task of enumerating the advantages of being a worrier. I've had to have something to look forward to. Following from the arguments in Chapter 3 that claim worry as the foundation for critical analyses of dominant political assumptions, Chapter 4 ponders more closely the sorts of minds that worry and asks whether there are blessings in the curse. Initially, I describe how my book itself betrays all the signs of the worrier—that it is worry-as-writing, writing-as-worry. But then I draw some strength from this by suggesting the analytical powers of the worrier's mind can be curiously beneficial and, despite everything, the odd basis for a kind of hope about how we might at least try to act by taking everything into account. I wonder about the strange gift of unhappiness that the worrier knows well and its role as a necessary counter to the glossy and glossing-over preference of contemporary cultures for superficial, individual-centered, cheeriness. Worriers, I suggest not entirely facetiously, could take on the happiness industry to our collective benefit. Beyond this assessment of the hidden "benefits" of worry as a practice of mind, I consider, finally, the failure of the self-help books to do much more than immerse a reader yet further into the self-centered choice culture that has exacerbated worry and given it more occasions to flourish than ever before. I assess, against this, what seems to me the furtive activities of the worrier to take strength from elsewhere. The second half of the chapter, that's to say, is about glimpsing alternatives to the worrier's world, with the emphasis on glimpse, on that which isn't too deeply known. The last part of this book is a cautious celebration and, in the end, a grateful one.

This final portion considers the way in which worriers can draw temporary consolation from the contentment of others as well as from objects and visual art. I think about the attraction of photographs as "anxiety-free" spaces; I examine the appeal of historical locations where, if worry once was, it isn't any longer. From this, I move on to suggest that literature—written word art—is less good at distracting the worrier simply because it's made from words. Rather, I assert, visual and musical forms propose better alternatives to worry because they are, at the deepest level, alternative *structures*: they possess an architecture that's a counter to the patterns and shapes of worry in the mind. I reflect on some sculptures and the heard reassurances of counterpoint in the music of J. S. Bach (1685–1750) as formal alternatives and, in turn, distractions from or consolations for the troubled world of the worrier's mind. Such art works better than words because it does not *tell* us what to believe but allows us to believe it.

My final thought is that trying to "cure" worry is wasted labor even if it's not wholly free of results. Worry is inextricable from the world in which, as westerners, we now live. The best thing to do is to understand why. Of course, I don't mean that worrying is "only" cultural: that it "merely" comes from outside to torment us. I remind myself of this point and I acknowledge throughout this book the personal and individual circumstances that interact with external factors to create the conditions for worry in any individual's life. We worriers have private stories to tell. And our private histories are not irrelevant. Some forms of help *can* make life better for us. Those forms are to be cherished and celebrated. But I want to move away from the assumption that being a worrier is *just* a matter of having something wrong with me, something personal or distinctive in my own history. And in turn I want to move away from the overwhelming assumption in contemporary print culture that worry is simply something that can be cured—whether by a therapist, a priest, a self-help book, or a bottle of Muscadet. I want to move away from a straightforward notion that we worriers have only ourselves to blame for worrying even if I'm periodically ready to rebuke us for ego and vanity. Actually, I'm often ready to do that. As will be clear, there are serious problems for me with the ethics of writing on worry and I'll face some conspicuous contradictions in my approach soon enough. But the central point remains. If we can't "cure" worry, we can venture to understand it—for better or for worse.

There's an element of fatalism in this book. The nineteenth-century critic and poet Matthew Arnold (1822–88) thought that the function of criticism (and he admitted "criticism" in the wide sense of "critical thinking") was "to see the object as in itself it really is."[3] That's a hard task in any area of our lives and often best avoided. Judgment is clouded, biased, obscured, and often or not based on a partial grasp of the evidence. But such effort at critical thinking is the ambition of this short book where worry is concerned. So doing, *Worrying* offers an account of the inner life as a tangle of trouble that's almost embarrassing to admit—almost embarrassing to *print*. We have relatively recently learned that a sophisticated inner life may be a marker of a complex and sophisticated individual. We've come to think, partly as a bequest of literary Modernism, that the quality of our inner sensitivities and private, undisclosed reflections on the world are indexes of our distinction and worth as individuals. Anglo-American and Irish Modernist narrative at the beginning of the twentieth

---

[3]Matthew Arnold, "The Function of Criticism in the Present Time," *Essays in Criticism* (London: Macmillan, 1865), p. 1.

century persuaded us that the possession of rich inner lives—Virginia Woolf's Mrs Dalloway, James Joyce's Leopold Bloom—indicates the significance of human personalities. We've become convinced that the possession of a rich, complex, or complicated inner life is what makes us interesting as people.

But worry isn't part of an inner life that makes for engaging or sophisticated narratives. Worrying's remote from a world of intriguing complications or glamorous desires and fascinating hopes. It's far from a definition of classy sensitivity or admirable psychological knottiness. Worry's a part of individuality, a feature of the inner life, about which we hardly dare talk. This is an inner life—looked at "as in itself it really is"—of which we can hardly be proud. And, if that inner life contains desires, they are for such humdrum and pale things as some peace and reassurance; some security and some time off from our own minds. The inner life of worry is one of discomfort, awkwardness, a loss of focus, a sense of dislocation, and an inability to accept the logic of the "most likely" in the eddies of faith in the improbable. The Modernists imaginatively engaged with worry as a feature of the interior mental spaces they represented. They brought worry into literature as a complex subject. But it's a more haggard form of bother that, for the most part, I'm looking at in this book. My business is, mostly, with a less attractive and less "sophisticated" form of mental activity than is usually brought trembling into the daylight. Marxists may claim that the idea of a fraught inner life of upset and distraction is merely indicative of the kinds of fragmented and anxious selves to which late capitalism has reduced us. There is truth in that, I guess, and I'm not blind to the role of economics in worry. Freudians may tell us that worries are only the tip of a terrifying iceberg: below the ordinary worry lies the deepest of psychological trauma. There may be truth in *that* though it's hard to test; it's difficult to step outside Freudian terms once you are in them. But what's of interest to me is the challenge of trying to talk about this hidden, resistant topic that's kept itself largely out of print for so long and of trying to see what *other* great cultural issues worry reveals to us about the way we live now. There's no sentimental version or vision of the mind in this book. There isn't a claim for the sophistication of the lives we worriers lead in our heads. I'm looking at a rough patch of land, covered with clumps of nettles and broken Muscadet bottles. I am interested in it because I live on it.

1

But woe is me, you are so sick of late

Hamlet, 3:2:156[1]

"Worry" doesn't have good synonyms. Anyone would think that English speakers didn't very often need the concept. "What's the matter with you?" "Well, you see, I am worried." That's not *necessarily* the same thing as saying, "I am anxious," though it's related. Sometimes, in fact, "anxiety" will do as well as "worry" in my discussion because both relate to states of mind troubled about the future. "Worry" is, more clearly, not the same as saying, "I am dispirited"; and certainly not the same thing as saying, "I am depressed." Worry is a form of fretfulness, of mental uncertainty and persistently tremulous bother. Worry is a form—of *worry*. What other word will, exactly, do?

This book has had some trouble getting off the ground. It has, in fact, been a source of considerable worry. Different readers have wanted it to be different. One reader wanted it to trace the fashioning of a concept of worry through Sigmund Freud and later psychoanalysts as if a great effort of academic study, through the

---

[1]All references to Shakespeare are to *The Oxford Shakespeare: The Complete Works*, 2nd edn, ed. Stanley Wells and Gary Taylor (Oxford: Oxford University Press, 2005).

history of psychoanalysis, would sort out what worry was and what to do about it. Worry, this person thought, needed to be rooted in an understanding of trauma, separation, and loss of the womb as Freud would no doubt have said. One reader, differently, wanted a book that analyzed all the diagnostics that appear in the mental health professional's catalog of symptoms, the fifth volume of the *Diagnostic and Statistical Manual of Mental Disorders* (DSM-5), issued by the American Psychiatric Association as a classification system for all mental disorders. This person thought that my book should trace "worry" from a clinical point of view and work out what *should* be in DSM-5. This was the manual, incidentally, which till 1974 described homosexuality as a mental disorder. It's not the neutral scientific manual some would like it to be.

Another reader thought that my project was misconceived from the start and should be about clinical anxiety—actual orders that *are* in DSM-5—and therapies to relieve it. "Worry" as a concept didn't seem to mean anything to them. Other readers lost interest when I revealed that my book wasn't about a pathological state but, mostly, an everyday one; a habit of thinking that keeps falling out of any formal definition of "mental illness." I was cheered up, even as I was being challenged, by the realization that there were so many people out there who didn't appear to recognize "worry." These people do not recognize what worry it is! Things are not as bad as I thought.

It's easy to see why worry is not often talked about—and not simply because English speakers appear to have so few words for it. "I am depressed" certainly would interest a clinician, let alone "I am suicidally unhappy." But "I am a worrier"? What are hard-pressed doctors or psychologists supposed to do with that? What are hard-pressed *friends* supposed to do with that? "Well, pull yourself together. Don't be so self-indulgent. Haven't you got more important things to be thinking about, let alone *writing* about?"

Worry has two other obvious features that help keep it out of conversation—and that's after I've suggested some kind of outline of what it is, which I haven't yet. Worry is, often or not, boring. And it's almost always embarrassing—even mortifying. We keep it to ourselves because it turns other people off and makes them think less of us. "Oh, there he is, worrying about that again . . . how tedious. How embarrassing. How *unmanly*." Talking about our worries is antisocial. It is dull.

WLTM someone who is not a worrier.

What we don't talk about can be a good topic of conversation. Out of the long catalog of things we do not, generally, consider in public as socialized human beings the topic of "my worries" could hardly be more obtrusively silent. "For all that the world," says the United States novelist Philip Roth wisely in his novel about racism, *The Human Stain* (2000), "is full of people who go around believing they've got you or your neighbor figured out, there really is no bottom to what is not known."[2] My book's a kind of footnote to that perception, a gloss, an example. I sometimes wonder, gloomily, about that deathbed moment when nothing more is to be done, nothing more to be lived, nothing more to be said. How many of us will die with matters of importance to our lives unmentioned, undiscussed, untold. Darkness will come down and nothing will be known of parts of our lives. Love for another; guilt for a crime; some shameful truth? Will we have forgotten to confess something or forgive someone we care about a wrong? Will we decide to take a grimy, reprehensible, or even criminal truth to the grave? There are such secrets, such truths, no doubt. But one thing definitely dies with worriers. The long list of hidden fears and troubles with which we have been negotiating all our life enters oblivion. And how much of our lives—at least for some of us—comprise such subterranean

---

[2]Philip Roth, *The Human Stain* (London: Vintage, 2005), p. 315.

anxieties? Worry's history is hard to write partly because most of the evidence is gone—thankfully, perhaps. Philip Roth thinks that men don't really know each other until they have admitted how much they think about sex. But who admits their worries?

This is a book that looks at a condition of the mind yet doesn't want merely to think of it in single or prepacked terms. *Worrying* doesn't only concern, say, pathology or medicine or counseling or therapy or worry's representations in literature and film or the history of psychoanalysis. I'm attempting to write about worry from different and more personal perspectives because worry is too complicated, and too important, just to be seen from one. This book isn't meant to be a cold formal study, a comprehensive account of one dimension of a great but buried human trouble. Yet a consequence of this disinclination to take any single approach is that I've no handy, ready-made methodology to tackle my subject. This book isn't a literary study of worry's representations, though it is partly that. It's not simply a study of the history of worry and its patterns, though it is partly that. It is not a self-help book about how to "cure" worry, and it is *definitely* not that. I have no easy model to follow.

My parameters aren't clear and my topic is fuzzy. Is *Worrying* a book about mental health in any meaningful way, I ask myself? It's become a familiar argument that "mental illness" needs to be, often or not, in scare quotes. "Mental illness" is, it's long been argued, created in part by an act of categorization. Mental illness exists in and through an act of perception. "Perhaps," says the controversial British psychologist Richard P. Bentall, "the line between sanity and madness must be drawn relative to the place at which we stand. Perhaps it is possible to be, at the same time, mad when viewed from one perspective and sane when viewed from another."[3] That's

---

[3]Richard P. Bentall, *Madness Explained: Psychosis and Human Nature*, new edn (London: Penguin, 2004), p. 117.

an unsettling thought—one that irritates some people—and its reverberations are enormous. Such illness, on this model, is not a fixed and definite state of actuality, which is uncontroversial and incontrovertible. Such illness is, in part, a decision made by one person about another. And that decision is based on evidence that can always be revised, re-perceived, challenged. But without saying too much about this conceptual issue yet, I have to ask is *worry* a matter of "mental health"? Do our current models of mental health have much room to talk about this kind of underground, furtive problem? Does worrying look more like a mental health issue from one perspective or another? Can we catalog it with any surety even if we can hardly talk about it?

Some scholars have begun the task of writing the cultural history of diseases and illnesses. This has happened more from university humanities departments than medical faculties. And that's seemed, primarily to the medical profession, a controversial matter and often wrong-headed. Writing a *history* of a disease implies that it has changed and not merely chemically or physiologically. Writing a history suggests that to understand a form of sickness means seeing it in, and as part of, human culture. Composing such a study implicitly proclaims that an illness is not merely related to the body but to "society" (whatever that is); that illness and disease exist in part as social constructions as well as somatic events.

"[Can] a disease have a biography?"[4] asks Lennard J. Davis, considering what is now called obsessive compulsive disorder (OCD) and its relationship to our time. How come OCD is a relatively new category of complaint? Is the answer that medical science is always "progressing" and has only now diagnosed this condition? Or is it

---

[4]Lennard J. Davis, *Obsession: A History* (Chicago, IL: University of Chicago Press, 2008), p. 3.

more complicated than that? Does the real history of OCD involve
the slow emergence of the cultural as well as physiological conditions
that make this complaint, and its diagnosis, *possible*? Perhaps the same
could be said for, say, *anorexia nervosa* or *myalgic encephalomyelitis/*
chronic fatigue syndrome? Trying to write the biography of a disease,
Davis uses the notion of "bioculture," a term for the attempt to situate a
disease or illness in the complicated networks of human development.
Bioculture assumes diagnoses and labeling of complaints are the
products of a mixture of biology and history, of physiology and
human society. Accordingly, OCD and other forms of obsession strike
Davis, in his compelling study *Obsession: A History* (2008), as related
to the modern world's cultural obsession with obsession itself. OCD
is a condition possible only in a busy, driven, modern society where
obsessive behavior is more visible, more affirmed, more seemingly
necessary than ever before. Obsession is, at one level, created for and
by our time.

But worry isn't a disease. Our current categories of mental illness
have little space for the kind of worry that I am talking about. Worry
is part of the fabric of life so, well—there it is. How does worry relate
to a conception of *health*? If we can't be certain of that answer—
what does *health* here mean?[5]—we will struggle to place, to situate,
worry in quite the right sort of frame to analyze it. Can this not-
disease, this somehow-related-to-mental-health-but-not-a-mental-
illness, have a biography? I have an uncertain category of human
experience to examine with an uncertain methodology. What *am* I
doing? I have daunting questions about how the category of "mental
health" relates to worry; how worry relates to any new and fuller
understanding of what we, in the modern world, should understand

---

[5]Consider Adam Phillips's discussion of how infrequently the "opposite" of mental illness is
defined in *Going Sane* (London: Hamish Hamilton, 2005).

by "mental health" or "mental unhealth." So I start without a ready guide as to how to talk about this thing, how to study this thing, how to find words for a thing that is felt more than it is discussed, experienced more than analyzed. And for which there appear to be very few words—words that some lucky people apparently don't comprehend at all.

One thing's pretty sure. I am going to get this wrong. But I'm not going to worry about that too much. I am going to try. And I'm going to try because I really do want to bring worry into the conversation; I want to make it possible to begin to talk about it rather than just experience it. I want to use my experience of worry to prompt some questions about what we think of as mental health and "well-being"; about what we really think of the *inner life*. I want to find better ways of talking *about* the inner life and what happens and does not happen there (and I even want to think about the unpopular subject of whether we, actually, *have* an inner life in the way the Modernists told us). I want to begin to search out what it is we think we know of another person when we take worry into account. For a person's worries, locked away silently in the cell of their minds most of the time, can make them sharply, astonishingly, different from how they appear to others. Self-perception and "self-experience" can, because of worry, be starkly different from the self's perception by friends, colleagues, and families. So starkly different, it maybe, that human beings will struggle to find better day-to-day evidence of how little they know each other.

I'm bothered by the curious happenings in the attic of the mind and what we don't know about them. I want to find out why I worry, and, in doing so, to bring worry, as a strange part of the consciousness, into language. This book isn't simply a set of thoughts on worry's history, its literature, its meanings, its "cures"—though it is that in parts, as I've said. It is, certainly, an exploration of what could be called the "culture of worry": the whole social, theological, political, and aesthetic networks producing and labeling and giving meaning to worry. There *is* something of Davis's "bioculture" here, however inexact the match between his medicalized topic and my almost completely nonmedicalized. But my book isn't only about these things. This book is about a personal journey to find more about worry and what it means, both for good and bad. It's about worry as much as it's about me: Francis O'Gorman, worrier. Here's a someone who feels, sometimes, fragile, oversensitive, over-conflicted, fretful, sleepless. He feels, at times, like china in a bull shop. Not all the time by any means—but definitely some of the time. *Worrying* is, to this extent, an act of personal exposure, a comedy of mental manners and sometimes not much of a comedy. That's my best hope for achieving anything like authenticity about a topic that has so many obstacles and no settled methodology to speak of but which constitutes a presence that's vividly alive to me inside the untidiness of my private mental space.

I'd like to be able to say that I wrote this book for others who, like me, sometimes struggle to see clearly through rainy windows of worry. I'd like to say that *Worrying* is intended to help all of those who can't quite clear things up, sort things out, in worrying minds. I'd like to say that it is a book for reading in the middle of sleepless nights. But in fact it is only in one general sense written with an intention to help; with a belief that it can be of any therapeutic use at all. That intention will become clear by the end. More generally, and in every other way, this book assumes and tries to prove that worry can't be cleared up given where we all are and who we are. A while ago, I described this book as I was writing it to a friend. He listened patiently, and rather skeptically. He finally said: "Is it like, then, some kind of literary self-help book?"

No. It's a kind of literary there's-no-help-book.

Some things can relieve worry, to be sure. Some things can take off the top soil. But worry's part of life as we know it now, down to the rocks.

I've used the word "worry" or a variant on it 162 times already (163 including that one). It's not a topic that makes for elegant writing because the same term keeps coming back. Using those not-quite-synonyms causes problems for the specificity of worry. But what *is* the specificity of worry? What, simply put, *is* it? What do I mean by worry? Even by the end of this book, I don't think I'll have pinned down all its meanings, placed it wholly in a glass cabinet with a label. I won't have caught all possible resonances or captured all the ways in which we, as human beings, now use the word "worry" in our efforts to describe how we feel and what our troubles are. Part of worry's nature is evasiveness. Language does not stick to it easily. Worry, like a bat, does not like being brought into the light. Worry keeps coming up with new alternative meanings for itself. It's fugitive from absolute and final definition not least because it is different to different people. "Worry," the word, flits in and out of day-to-day conversation with a host of different senses. Tracking worry down is a cumulative process and sometimes a clumsy one. Worry is a bit of a worrying word.

Here, though, are some first definitions—my working assumptions—concerning the principal ways in which I understand the term: what *I* mean when I describe a part of my inner life with the term "worry." Worry certainly has the habit of being partly included in other things (I guess my account of worrying about that meeting at the beginning of my book included a good deal of anger as well as worry). Worry is more easily accommodated in the ordinary and the familiar than the state of "being anxious," which has a hint of the clinician's label and is often ready to become extreme, disabling. It goes without saying that the worry in which I'm primarily interested fits into the ordinary, the functional, even the successful life, far better than depression.

Household, everyday, functional "worry" is ready and waiting, like a shadow, but it's not a pathological condition as I understand it. Anxiety sometimes implies a condition of mind that takes greater hold of a sufferer than worry—as if it is something flatter and squatter. "Anxiety" is a term more frequently used in relation to panic attacks, phobias, perfectionism, visible obsessions, antisocial behavior. That is not exactly the world of worry in which I'm interested. Ordinary worry rarely grips so hard that nothing else can happen, though sometimes worrying in the middle of the night can feel pretty desperate. "Fretfulness" is a comrade of worry and so is trepidation. Yet worry, most amply defined, still has senses that are peculiar to it. No other word will quite do for this mundane, subterranean, and persistent condition of the frowning, fretful modern mind that can hit me like a blast of cold air from a cave.

Worry can be collective but it's far more often personal. It's possible to describe a "national worry" (about the rise of Fascism, say, or the chances of a national team). It's possible to describe a global worry (such as climate change, nuclear war, or the survival of Chilean miners trapped below the earth). But worry is more characteristic and characterizable, simply more familiar, when it's an individual's problem. Worry has internal mental patterns and that can't easily be said of a whole nation or a whole planet. Personal worry can be spoken about aloud but it's more often kept secretly away in the mind. It is part of our underground life. It is part, perhaps, of that portion of our lives that we find it hard to believe that anyone else experiences—and hard to believe that they would believe *us* if we told them. Worry's primary nature is a concern about an unknown future or, more exactly, about a future that has *some element* of the uncertain in it. Its most habitual form for an individual is a question, sometimes literally, beginning with "*What if . . .?*"

Worry is circular. It may begin with a "simple" anxiety, a basic question. It can be as straightforward as "Did I lock the back door?" It is insistent—"Did I *really* lock the back door?"—and it has a nasty habit of taking off on its own, of getting out of hand, of spawning thoughts that are related to the original worry and which make it worse. This is where worry becomes—gulp—hard to admit. For that simple question can, without too much difficulty, skein out into disturbing possibilities. This whole book takes a single "simple" thing and worries *at* it. It exposes all the implications and hidden meanings and possibilities of worry in a way that's natural to a worrier. Like a fully paid-up worrier, I am making that simple, seemingly more-or-less manageable thing called "ordinary worry" into something very much worse, bringing to light hidden implications of a commonplace condition you probably never realized were there.

"If I *did* leave that back door open, we might be burgled." That might be the first of the characteristic supplementary developments of a simple worry. Then comes the mind's pursuit of all the potential consequences of one small error. "What about the burglar stealing my passport, or my memory stick, or my DVD collection, or *setting fire to the house?* I have read about that somewhere—." How hard it is to admit such things as they move onward from and into fearfulness as worry rumbles quietly away in the back of the mind, playing with *what might be.* This may all seem incredible or ridiculous. Actually, in a way, it *is* ridiculous. But if you are a worrier, I'm hoping you know what I am talking about.

Worry goes on remorselessly producing even more troubling versions of the consequences of the original question. It's an assessment of the possibilities born from a single thought. Worry works, typically, with a ruthless grasp of cause-and-effect and it is good at producing bad chains of "what happens next." Of course, the starting point can be obviously dark, much more threatening than the possible consequences of possibly having left the back door open.

It's worth being clear about this.

Worry is often mildly or reasonably painful; sometimes it is very painful. Those who are not habitually worriers will no doubt face serious matters for worry at some point. I'm a habitual worrier and one of the many things I struggle with is putting into order, putting into a hierarchy of priorities, what I am worried about. If I think I *have* left the back door open, I don't always discriminate between the seriousness of that problem with one that's graver: a friend's illness, for instance; my doubts that higher education is going to survive in any decent form in England. It's not always the gravity of the thing worried about that determines how worried the worrier is; how sore the worry. Many who are not habitual worriers worry at times. Life's too difficult, troubled, and worrying not to. But I'm mostly concerned here with the habits of the regular worrier's mind, with worry as an everyday and even banal condition. The broad patterns of worry for the occasional worrier, faced with a difficult and uncertain future, nevertheless, are the same.

One of the most common kinds of everyday worry is particularly bleak because it's the mind worrying about the body. It is what used to be called, a few years ago, "hypochondria," the *malade imaginaire* of the seventeenth-century French playwright Molière (1622–73). "Hypochondria" is now more frequently known in contemporary medicine by various polite circumlocutions: somatic distress; medically unexplained symptoms; somatization; or subthreshold, subsyndromal, or nondiagnosable distress. Those sound less threatening: they sound more like a reassuringly scientific certainty than a criticism. But they all describe a problem that, as a form of worry, starts with a single, "simple," and identifiable question about the body: "Could this pain in my head be something bad?" "Does the fact I feel so tired mean I have something really wrong with me?" "Does that new mole indicate anything serious?" These don't have to go far down a chain of cause-and-effect to come right up against imagined calamity.

The history of the word "hypochondria" offers some insight into the emergence of the more general "worry" in modern language. The early Victorian novelist Charlotte Brontë (1816–55) is one of English literature's most remarkable narrators of a form of mental distress she called "hypochondria," which was, in her day, a more general term for unrooted fretfulness. Brontë doesn't offer an analysis of this condition. But she does describe what it feels, and looks, like with some dexterity. In her novel about an English schoolteacher in Belgium, *Villette* (1853), Charlotte Brontë figures the life-depriving results of a continual fretfulness, the capacity of worry to take cheer away. Lucy Snowe, the novel's depressed heroine, attends a concert and sees the monarch of Labassecour (Charlotte was always rude about Belgium in *Villette*: the name means "the barn yard"). He's clearly a man of sorrows. "There sat a silent sufferer," Lucy observes:

> —a nervous, melancholy man. Those eyes had looked on the visits of a certain ghost—had long waited the comings and goings of that strangest spectre, Hypochondria. Perhaps he saw her now on that stage, over against him, amidst all that brilliant throng. Hypochondria has that wont, to rise in the midst of thousands— dark as Doom, pale as Malady, and well-nigh strong as Death. Her comrade and victim thinks to be happy one moment—"Not so," says she; "I come." And she freezes the blood in his heart, and beclouds the light in his eye.[6]

Perfectly captured is fretfulness's habit of returning, its circularity, its refusal to be put off with an answer. Brontë's "hypochondria" makes

---

[6]Currer Bell [Charlotte Brontë], *Villette* (London: Smith, Elder, 1889), pp. 216–7.

something of the shape of modern worry clear. Modern worry is made from questions: perhaps the "I come" of worry's return, back with the same inquiry. Worrying involves a kind of mental risk assessment gone wrong. It can make the most unlikely outcome the most intrusive, visible, and important. It confuses prioritization and inhibits an ability to decide what's likely. What theoretically *could* happen is not the best basis for working out what will. The worrier's questions are distinctive because, although they can often technically be answered, the worrier doesn't admit, or at least for very long, the reliability of an answer. Worry doesn't *like* answers. It has something tyrannical about it. Worriers don't respond well to being interrogated.

It's unfortunate then, that the best way to respond to someone's worries often seems to be: answer the worrier's questions. Explain the most likely outcome. Show them the illogicality or improbability of what they're worrying about. Often or not, the answering technique begins with a counter-assertion: "I am sure you didn't leave that door open"; "I am sure there is nothing serious about your headache." Sometimes, that is as far as the respondent gets. But worriers can rarely be calmed by the mere statement of the opposite that concerns them (which is a pity, since it is a staple technique of the nonworrier's advice to the worrier).

Next may well come a better effort to answer: a reasoned response: "Anyway, is there not a back *gate* that will be locked so no one could get into the garden anyway?" Now this is credible and sensible. But, alas, there is likely to be a way round it. For, typically, the worrier has gone through this already in his or her own mind. He or she certainly does not say, "Oh yes, you are right. Silly me," and pack in thinking about that door. Even if the worrier temporarily finds some respite in that new perspective—when it *is* new—he or she is soon in trouble again. "Well, there *is* a gate at the bottom of the garden . . . but it is not difficult to climb over particularly if there are two of you"; "Well, there *is* a gate at the bottom of the garden, but the lock is feeble and, actually, you can lean on the gate . . ." The trouble has not gone away. Worry has found the gate closed and gone round the side.

Worry's favorite shape is a circle. It may seem that these long chains of cause-and-effect are straight lines, moving far beyond the original starting point. But, in fact, they're loops. They come back to themselves. The worrier's mind is one that can take a break from worrying chiefly by distraction, by temporarily forgetting about the worry. But as soon as the distraction is over, the worry starts over again as if there had never been "answers" to the questions after all.

That's why worry can be so exasperating to others. You think you're making progress with a worrier then, the next time you speak, you're back where you started. "How can you *still* be worrying about the same thing?!" "Didn't I explain that headache as probably too much coffee?" "Didn't I say you probably left your mobile phone at home, not on the car seat, like you did last time?" "Oh *really* don't worry about what you said to your sister, I'm *sure* she hasn't taken offense." But it's rarely much use saying anything like this—or much use for long. These are words that friends and families necessarily speak. They have to be spoken for there are no other words to use. They are the staple languages for dealing with worriers. They're the clichés of well-meant and sometimes irritated care. And they are usually useless. Such words are consumed, chewed up, and set to one side by the worrier—absorbed in a need for reassurance that can always be given and never be given for long. Worriers don't approve of answers because, in the end, we don't believe them. Our faith is elsewhere. There's no point in getting cross. It's not the fault of the friend who is trying to help.

That's just the way worriers are.

Worry often happens—almost always happens—while something else is going on. One of the simplest reasons why we don't talk about worry is because there's always something else to talk about.

It's perfectly possible, indeed absolutely normal, for worry to lurk beneath activities and other words. Worry goes on in the everyday and beneath the surface. Worriers are, for the most part, functional. They do not, generally, look like Charlotte Brontë's King of Labassecour. They look like you and me. Well, they certainly look like me. When the worrier lies awake at night fretting about her sister's health or the consequences of his next pay review, these are occasions when worry has got the worrier to itself. It may be that any really significant life is one that can only be understood as an allegory. But the continual allegory of the worrier's life, at its most extreme, is the meeting of Sensitivity and Trepidation, Insecurity and the omens of Some Great Problem. Worry *can* be center stage. Worry can have almost total possession of the worrier's mind. But, more often than not, worry's only one occupant of mental space. Worry's favorite shape may be the circle. Yet it also has to accommodate things on top of each other. There's something geological about worry. It lurks in layers beneath the surface.

The worrier might easily be in a conversation at work and still worrying. To all intents and purposes, everything looks normal and, for the worrier, everything pretty much *is* normal. This is how things are. The scene might run a little like this:

Worrier. Did you say we had overspent on office equipment this quarter? (if that I can't get home quickly tonight I don't know how I'm going to finish the preparation for the presentation tomorrow).

Other. I'm afraid so.

W. Was most of it on those new computers we bought? (That presentation could go badly without proper preparation and I have left it so late; if it goes badly, we might lose that contract and all the money that we are expecting.)

O. And the new desks.

W. Well, at least those will last us a few years (I shouldn't be stuck here on this minor problem with last quarter's spending on office furniture but able to get on with writing that presentation: if it doesn't work and I think it would have been better if I had had more time, I'd only have myself to blame . . .)

That's a clue. Yet worry is hard to communicate, to get down on paper, perfectly. Here are representations rather than replications. That problem's always at the heart of trying to understand what is happening in another's mind, particularly where anything as wordless as pain is concerned. It's a problem here. Two "lines" of meaning "occur" at the same time and, of course, there may be others lingering: "I need some coffee" might be slowly stretching across the speaker's mind beneath or through both these strands of thought. "My gout hurts." But, in my representation, the reader can only read one line, one word, at a time. Representation necessarily compromises, recasts, mediates the experience the words are describing. Worry pulses quietly under spoken, audible language and other words, intending to describe this, misrepresent the at-the-same-time-ness of what worry is like. Simultaneity, the quiet intrusiveness of worry, its woodpecker-like tapping away at one's day from inside the unobservable parts of the mind, can be gestured toward in language. But the experience can't be transparently repeated through it.

The Anglo-American Modernist poet T. S. Eliot (1888–1965) was a worrier himself and a writer on worry. I think he was worry's first poet.[7] He imagined these layers of anxiety with an apt turn of phrase. Eliot's early poem, "Portrait of a Lady" (1917), described a concert,

---

[7]See Francis O'Gorman, "Modernism, T.S. Eliot, and the 'Age of Worry,'" *Textual Practice*, 26 (2012), pp. 1001–19.

which was suggestive of empty fashionability, of the vacuousness of supposedly cultured high-class lives. But the speaker, like the King of Labassecour, is only half attending to the music (what *is* it about concerts and worry?). Anxiety is beating a mental tattoo. "Inside my brain," Eliot's narrator says, "a dull tom–tom begins."[8] The music is drowned by the inner percussion. That notion of a repetitive anxiety, a monotone or a monotheme, plays on Eliot's name (Thomas Stearns Eliot, known as Tom) as if to suggest the double self: the outward social self and the inner troubled self. That choice of words hints at the uncomfortable idea that selfhood, the *real* Tom, comes from and with the fretfulness of an inner life made from repeats that will not go away. Tom and the tom–tom are inseparable: they help make each other what they are.

If I can describe, most of the time, what my worry is, does that mean somehow worry *actually happens* in words in my head (or is it more like a wordless "tom–tom" of pain)? Do actual words float through my mind, describing my worry, constituting my worry? Do I think in language about worry? Do I worry *in English*?

I think I need to say something about that phrase "rational and logical." Worry almost always deals with the *possible*, however unlikely. Or, at least, it deals with what's possible *according to the worrier's understanding*. A friend of mine worried about aircraft travel because she thought that there was only a vacuum above the clouds—that there was nothing for a plane to be supported by, as a ship is supported by water. This she believed faithfully for many years. She was unflappable in her conviction that this is how things were. Not a shred of any science suggested differently to her. As a consequence, she would not fly because she thought that an airplane, if it traveled too slowly, would simply fall out of the sky. There was nothing to support it. Then my

---

[8]T. S. Eliot, *Collected Poems 1909–1962* (London: Faber, 1974), p. 19.

friend discovered, or was finally persuaded, that there was more than emptiness above the clouds—there was *air*. Thin air, it is true, but air nevertheless. Reassured by this realization, she worried less about accidents. My friend thought of planes as somehow on cushions.

The point, here, is not that any of this is scientifically accurate or inaccurate. The point is that the idea of a plane dropping out of the sky in a vacuum seemed to my friend possible and so, in her own conception of atmospheric science, it was. That's what I mean by "possible according to the worrier's understanding." Worry puts almost into words problems that are ones of possibility. The chains of cause-and-effect have plausibility—and the representation of these chains can be communicated in language that is, accordingly, understandable. That language follows familiar patterns of logic and causality even if the logic only *seems* to be logic. And yet, if those words are understandable, if they follow semi-logical patterns, are they *exactly what worry is*? Worry as it happens in the head can be spoken about in words. But what is its actual relationship to language? When I worry about whether the back door is open or not (I just went downstairs to check), do actual words like "*is the back door shut?*" form in my mind—*really*?

I wish I could catch myself worrying and then stand back and watch. But the truth is I can't definitely answer my own question about worry and words because—I can't stand back and watch. Like sleep, worry happens when I'm not ready to observe it. I'm forced to talk about past worries even if they are only a few seconds past. There's a larger philosophical question here about the relationship between thought and words, about the relationship between language and the shape as well as the act of thinking, which I'm not competent to understand. But as far as worry is concerned, I know there're two things worth underlining in this awkward *pas-de-deux* between fretfulness and language. The first is simply that worry's near-relationship with words—the fact that we *can* say, very often, what we are worried about—should not mislead us into thinking that worry is only words, or that, as words, it can easily be part of a dialogue or a discussion. Worrying has a close relationship with language because it mimics the patterns of logical analysis and in this sense it is *possible* to talk about and to represent. But worry can't merely be "retold" in language. Worry's always something other than the words by which it's known to others.

Second, this conception of mental pain that is always semi-fugitive from language is a problem for any conception of therapy and, beyond the notion of worry, the relationship between pain and words is a key difficulty for the whole realm of mental health and mental suffering. Mental health, most broadly defined, peculiarly relies on acts of representation. There's material evidence in the brain for some kinds of diagnosis and the medical professions, in conjunction with advanced technology, hope to define more. But the matter is controversial. What, indeed, can matter tell us? Brain scans of a "normal brain" and of an OCD brain, for instance, certainly look different.[9] But what kind of knowledge does such imaging really provide? "What [such] pictures actually show," says the American novelist and poet Siri Hustvedt appositely in her investigation of the relationship between brain and self, *The Shaking Woman or A History of My Nerves* (2009): "and how to read them, remains controversial." "Time and again," Hustvedt continues, "I have heard scientists articulate their doubts about what the images actually *mean*, and yet the pictures are often called upon as evidence." And when such images enter popular newspapers and media, they are indeed "mostly cleansed of the doubt that surrounds them."[10] That is right. These things become images

---

[9]See, for instance, p. 27 of Davis's *Obsession*.
[10]Siri Hustvedt, *The Shaking Woman or a History of My Nerves* (New York: Henry Holt, 2009), p. 33.

of apparently materialist truth, remote from the caution, doubt, and uncertainty with which they were born. Images need words to explain them. And mental pain, with or without the evidence of images, needs more words. Knowing the inside of the head is principally a matter of language, of talking. Either the pictures don't tell us everything or there simply aren't any pictures. There are no scans to show what a *worrying* brain looks like. So we have to *tell* someone else what's happening in our minds and thus we are forced into words. Worriers, like sufferers from many different forms of mental pain, are likely to be assessed, responded to, and even treated on the basis not of what is wrong with them but on how good they are at describing it.

It may seem that worry fits with relative ease into descriptive words and, as such, is distinct from other forms of mental pain. The experience of depression, for instance, is barely possible to put into any kind of language without significant loss; without conspicuous awareness of how far language is not communicating to the listener what the sufferer is enduring. "Until one has experienced a debilitating severe depression," says the developmental biologist Lewis Wolpert in *Malignant Sadness: The Anatomy of Depression* (1999), "it is hard to understand the feelings of those who have it." What can words do with, and how do we explain, these feelings?

> Severe depression borders on being beyond description: it is not just feeling much lower than usual. It is a quite different state, a state that bears only a tangential resemblance to normal emotion. It deserves some new and special word of its own, a word that would somehow encapsulate both the pain and the conviction that no remedy will ever come. We certainly could do with a better word for this illness than one with the mere common connotation of being "down."[11]

---

[11]Lewis Wolpert, *Malignant Sadness: The Anatomy of Depression* (London: Faber, 1999), p. 1.

Worry is easier to speak and write about than that. It doesn't primarily
need new words: it just needs more words. And, if those words fall
short, they're closer to revealing what's going on in the mind than
the broken shards of vocabulary and splinters of syntax that try to
describe depression or communicate the lows of "bipolarity."[12] I can
get *some* understanding of what's worrying you. Language and pain
have a better relationship here.

Worry, then, as I've defined it so far, is a species of *trepidation* about
an *uncertain future*. It is, almost always, some version of a question
about security (sometimes literally when that wretched back door's
concerned). Worry's something *different from words* yet it has a *close
relationship* to them—closer, to be sure, than some other elements of
diagnosable mental illness. Worry can best be *represented* in words, in
its most characteristic form, as a *set of questions* about the future that
generate imagined chains of *cause-and-effect*. Worry deals with what's
plausible to the worrier and, in this sense, is a *form of logic* working
inside set premises. It does not respond well to "logical" responses to
its own logic, though, and is good at inventing plausible reasons for
returning to fretfulness. Worry is usually *circular* and it's quite able
to happen *while other things occur* in the worrier's mind. It very often
does.

Worry, as I'm talking about it here, belongs with the stuff of
normal life, as much as normal life provides the substance *for* worry. I
shouldn't be ambiguous about this. I've said that worry, in its regular
state, hardly interests the clinician. Men and women visit the doctor
because they have something worrying them. But how many go with
the worry itself? "Doctor, is there anything you can do to help me stop
worrying?" "Worrying about what, exactly?" "No, just worrying—I

---

[12]On the problems with that term, see Kay Redfield Jamison's *An Unquiet Mind: A Memoir
of Moods and Madness* (New York: Knopf, 1995).

would like to be cured of it." Worrying in its usual manifestations is not a pathological condition. There are no tablets for it, no cream. I doubt that there are any patients sitting in a hospital bed anywhere in the world at this moment because, and only because, they're ordinary worriers.

Mental health professionals don't have a familiar category for worry (though I imagine that there are plenty of doctors' notes where "Bit of a worrier" is scribbled on them about this patient or that—probably including mine). Of course, there's worry gone out of control. There is ordinary worry—and extraordinary. There's worry in an excessive form that dominates a life so much that it prohibits almost everything else. That is a grave condition and a serious form of mental illness, of the sort that *does* reach the pages of DSM-5. "Acute Anxiety Disorder," the bitter forms of debilitating and extreme fearfulness, is ordinary worry made grotesque. The worry that is my concern isn't normal life's grim opposite. It's certainly not normal life's nemesis. *My* worry is, for the most part, exactly that which happens while normal life does too. It doesn't make life exactly easy but it certainly doesn't stop it.

It's actually possible to worry *about worrying*, by the way, since it's possible to worry that worrying *will* stop normal life. Emily Colas's autobiography *Just Checking: Scenes from the Life of An Obsessive-Compulsive* (1998) is a witty account of the difference between, and the movement from, "ordinary" worry to an OCD. It makes for unnerving reading for a regular, day-to-day, household worrier. It makes me worry—if I allow myself—about becoming *this* type of worrier. The early twentieth-century writers on worry were inclined to think that worry was only the first stage on a downhill slide to mental breakdown or awful psychological problems, as total abstainers are sometimes inclined to think that someone who takes a single glass of wine will end up on a bottle of methylated spirits a day and living in the gutter. *Just Checking* runs some risk of persuading me, against my better judgment, that there just might be something in that view. Colas's initial pattern of worries is, worryingly enough, not wholly removed from ordinary secret fears. Emily Colas knows there is something awry, something strange happening to her, when she frets in a restaurant about the fact that the waiter is wearing a Band-Aid, a plaster. Her husband tries to find out what his injury is to stop his wife worrying. The waiter says he hurt himself helping a friend move house. "I looked at my husband," Colas writes:

> Unconvinced. "What if he was lying? Trying to cover for potentially infecting us?"
>
> "He seems like a pretty honest guy," my husband answered.
>
> "I wonder how long ago this happened?"
>
> Here's my thinking. If the injury occurred a few days ago, then the cut was probably scabbed. Not as dangerous. But if it were more recent, then who knows, maybe it was leeching fluid. "Ask him . . ." I stopped talking. I realized I have a talent. I possess an endless capacity to keep a worry alive."[13]

This capacity becomes a talent to destroy. Colas slips from this mildly obsessive fretting into serious problems that are mainly based around hygiene and cleaning. Her life becomes dominated, almost constituted, by her obsessive checking and worrying and vacuuming. Drugs, in the end, help. It's an extreme story. But ordinary worriers, if we're not determined, might shudder a little in recognizing something of that talent, the capacity to keep worries alive, even in the midst of our own daily lives. Might we go this way too . . .

---

[13]Emily Colas, *Just Checking: Scenes from the Life of An Obsessive-Compulsive* (New York: Pocket Books, 1998), p. 33.

Fortunately regular day-to-day worriers, most of the time, just stay as we are. We don't get much worse and we don't get much better. Emily Colas *isn't* who we become. There can be much more minor matters. Although worry characteristically is a set of questions, leaking out from an initial trepidation, worry can be very much briefer. In this less distinct form, when there's just a pulse of local anxiety that doesn't begin to multiply, worry nestles closer to the day-to-day. These kinds of worries are forms of pain that don't last long. They're quickly distracted. These beats, taps, and twinges are, typically, something like a momentary worry about where my wallet is or whether the milk has run out in the fridge or whether I put a stamp on that letter I posted earlier in the morning. They're tiny and fleeting. They are simply part of the pattern or texture of the worrier's day—here and gone. But, while they look on paper like the regular thoughts of anyone during a regular day, these thoughts are attended for the worrier by something darker, more out-of-keeping with their apparent insignificance. These little thoughts are not neutral, not emotion-free ideas that flap through the mind like a sparrow through a mead hall. These little worries come with a sense of dull disquiet; a momentary flash of the very mildest panic; a twinge of real unease; an actual, but brief, quickening of the pulse. Even the most minor of troubles can, for the worrier—hurt.

That's the other thing to be clear about in this effort to pin down what worry is. Worry is pain. It is usually pain without clear end, too, because if time proves one worry to be unfounded ("Oh, thank heavens, I *did* lock that door . . .") then there is another ready shortly afterward (". . . but what about that meeting tomorrow?"). My attempt to tell the history of worry isn't meant to make pain go away or to pretend it doesn't exist. I'm not attempting somehow to show that worry is "only" a product of culture rather than an actual, real ache in the mind.

. . . how I wish . . .

Has worry *always* been with us? Or is it just the case that it has not always had that name? Worry may seem a natural part of the day-to-day, a part of the mental furniture of the twenty-first century in the West. But its modern form reached the present through a process. It has a back story. In fact, as far as I can see, it has several. Each history that can be told about worry is incomplete without another, though all the histories cannot all be told at the same time. Like worry itself, worry's histories are in layers. As there are different kinds of worry, so there are different kinds of history. The back story of worry is rolled up with the history of ideas, with medical history, with the emergence of advanced capitalism, with great shifts in our understanding of theology, with changes in a comprehension of what the "self" is and what is private about it. The history of worry belongs with the history of human selfhood and of what makes a person. It's part of the broadest sweep of our past and we still have hardly anything that suffices for a critical method to bring such material together. Those histories take a reader into some of the most important questions about contemporary living and our relationship with the forces that made us. Worry's histories, as I'm going to suggest, are to do with nothing less than the structure of the modern world; with shifts in the understanding of the rules by which human beings make decisions; with the drift of the West toward the secular; with the dislodging and relocation of faith and what we believe in and what we think faith does; with a whole flourishing and deeply misunderstood, highly politicized notion of what is human "freedom" and the importance of "choice." These all add up to the forces which, outside the mind, shape the inside of it.

They account for The Way We Worry Now.

But there's a "local" or "short" history too. This is the story of worry's appearance as a word: its entry into discourse, its appearance in writing, its availability as a label for human beings to describe their lives. Worry as a state of mind may have a history that stretches back to the beginning of human consciousness. But it's first named, in the form we know it today, by the Victorian period.

Of course, it's hard to believe that *something like worry* had not been experienced before the nineteenth century. I've more to say about this in Chapter 2. Did cave men "worry" about saber-toothed tigers hiding around the next rock? Did the architects of the Stonehenge "worry" that they had placed the stones in the slightly wrong place? Did soldiers lie awake at night before the Battle of Agincourt on October 25, 1415 fearing what might happen to them? It's difficult to imagine that they didn't. And yet how difficult it is to be certain that those feelings, the ways men and women thought in the past, can be exactly mapped onto contemporary ways of feeling and thinking. The history of human subjectivity is too complicated, too vast a matter, to begin to comprehend. What looks like "worry" to our generation may just be an easy imposition of our ways of being onto the different ways of being, of feeling, of possessing subjectivity in the past.

Judaeo-Christian scripture sometimes suggests states of mind that, to modern readers, *seem* like worry. But we can't whole-heartedly know if they are. 1 Kings 20:43, for instance, describes in the Authorized Version how "the king of Israel went to his house heavy and displeased, and came to Samaria." Being "heavy" might have some element of worry in it, perhaps? By the time of the easy-reading English of the *Good News Bible*, translated for the American Bible Society from 1966, some translators clearly thought it did. In the *Good News*, this line reads: "The king went back home to Samaria, worried and depressed." The king suddenly seems closer in time, a contemporary, "worried and depressed." In the New Testament, Jesus might be talking about something akin to worry in Luke 12:22 when he says to the disciples in the Authorized Version: "Therefore I say unto you, Take no thought for your life, what ye shall eat; neither for the body, what ye shall put on." That "thought" could be worry, perhaps? Again, *Good News* thought so. "Then Jesus said to the disciples," their translation runs, "And so I tell you not to worry about the food you need to stay alive or about the clothes you need for your body." "Worried" appears 33 times in the *Good News* version; "worry" 51. Neither word appears in the Authorized Version at all.

Yet new words don't easily describe old concepts. Is the difference between *Good News* and the Authorized Version a matter of language change or of conceptual change? And what's the relationship of both to the concepts active in the minds of the original Hebrew and Greek writers of the Old and New Testaments? If the word "worry" is helpful to the modern reader, we can hardly be sure how far the notion, the experience of worry, was comprehensible at different moments of distant history. Tracking a concept is hard.

But at least tracking a word is not.

Prior to the Victorians, the verb "to worry" existed in English. But it was not the same concept that it labeled. Worry, as a verb, referred to the act of choking or strangling, later of distressing, human beings or animals. It was about acts of physical harassment, sometimes leading to death. Shakespeare uses "worry" only once in his entire corpus of plays and poetry. And that is what he means. The moment occurs in his great, angry, mischievous, propagandist, pro-Tudor drama, *Richard III* (1592–3). Queen Margaret, in the harrowing scene 4 of Act 5 that dramatizes some of the human consequences of the loathsomeness of Richard, describes the king as "[a] hell-hound that doth hunt us all to death":

> That dog, that had his teeth before his eyes,
> To worry lambs and lap their gentle blood

(4:4:48–50)

A dog worrying a lamb: this is the king as worrier but in the pre-Victorian sense. This meaning remains available to us. Dogs still worry bones and if they are not on leashes in the countryside, they sometimes worry lambs. But Richard III, in Shakespeare's influential perception of him, has viciously "worried" living human beings into the grave.

How far does a word's appearance in recoverable written language, such as that which historical dictionaries use as evidence, precede or follow from a word's establishment in familiar spoken language, of which traces are lost? How far does a word's appearance precede or follow from the establishment of the *concept* it describes? As far as I can see, the change from Shakespeare's sense of worry to the modern meaning, insofar as it's documented in written language, occurred, roughly speaking, just after the middle of the nineteenth century. That is nearly a quarter of a millennium after Shakespeare's death. Worry was on its way to the modern sense in the novelist Anthony Trollope's moving story of a poor clergyman, the Reverend Josiah Crawley, wrongly accused of theft in *The Last Chronicle of Barset* (1867). This is an important novel about what we would now call "mental illness." But that, for now, isn't the point. Mr Robarts, a fellow minister and the parson of Framley, is obliged at one moment in the story to leave his horse outside in bad weather while making a visit. It's not a comfortable business. Mr Robarts doesn't like leaving his horse outside. He "had more horses than one before now," Trollope's narrator observes, glancing back to a story about an expensive horse told in the earlier novel, *Framley Parsonage* (1860–1):

> and had been thought by some to have incurred greater expense than was befitting in his stable comforts. The subject, therefore, was a sore one, and he was worried a little.[14]

---

[14]Anthony Trollope, *The Last Chronicle of Barset* (Harmondsworth: Penguin, 1986), pp. 222–3.

Mr Robarts, we're invited to see, is harassed, unsettled, by a thought—
aware of criticism and perhaps feeling guilty. "Worry" is the verb
that suggests the problem. "The subject" starts somewhere outside
the mind and comes *at* him, like a hornet at a picnic. The problem
gets *inside* his mind and buzzes around. This is being worried-at by
a thought.

Seven years earlier in Boston, Joseph E. Worcester's *A Dictionary
of the English Language* (1860) offered another sense of the word's
changing meaning when he defined "to worry" in a colloquial sense
to mean "indulge in idle complaining; to fret; to be troubled."[15] There
was a strong hint of disapproval in that "to indulge": Worcester is in
the background, wagging his figure. But this idea of *fretting*—whatever
else worry was—is not the same as for Shakespeare's Richard III, the
literal, physical worrier of metaphorical lambs. This worry is in the
mind, like Mr Robarts's troubles. Worrying has left the fields and
entered the head.[16]

Nineteenth-century psychology, generally speaking, was more
concerned with madness than anything else. Nothing like worry, as
far as I can tell, made it into regular discussions of disturbed minds
and, sometimes, the startlingly cruel treatments. Earlier maps of the
mind that used phrenology—the conviction that the shape of the skull
indicated features about the brain and, in turn, of character—didn't
create much space for anything like low-level worry either. "Love
of approbation," said the influential phrenologist George Combe in
1828, can sometimes, when unregulated, lead to a "fidgety anxiety

---

[15]Joseph E. Worcester, *A Dictionary of the English Language* (Boston, MA: Hickling, Swan, and Brewer, 1860), p. 1683.

[16]*Oxford English Dictionary*, electronic edition, worry, v., 7c. Cf. 7a, "To cause distress of mind to; to afflict with mental trouble or agitation; to make anxious and ill at ease. Chiefly of a cause or circumstance," with the earliest date of usage as 1822 (Hazlitt). "Worried" is only defined as "harassed, fatigued," in Noah Webster's *An American Dictionary of the English Language* (New York: Converse, 1830), p. 934.

about what others will think of us." And Combe was prepared to say that one of the differences between human beings and other animals was a "ceaseless anxiety and contemplation [of futurity]."[17] But the phrenological model didn't provide a very useful or extended way of plotting the nature of worry, of fidgety anxiety, because its aim was not to chart what the modern world calls the inner life. Phrenology was more interested in character traits than individual consciousnesses; more in what adjectives might apply to different "types" of human behaviors than what it felt like inside an individual's head.

As worry's name was beginning to be known in this new sense, it began to appear in imaginative accounts of human lives at the end of the Victorian period. The novelists, peculiarly interested in inside the mind, started to describe it. "I'm only a bit worried about things in general," says Dick Heldar, the beleaguered hero of Rudyard Kipling's first rather depressing novel, *The Light that Failed* (1891).[18] What painful irony of imprecision there is in that sentence: a worry *"about things in general."* This may be more of a low-level depression, perhaps. But a small cluster of what I would venture to call "worry novels," written at the end of the nineteenth century, largely documented ordinary lives trapped in difficult financial and domestic circumstances. Worry was, here, peculiarly attached to economic predicaments as if it were the distinctive offspring of the precarious need to earn a living; of the problematic relationship between challengingly competitive public demands and insecurity of mind.

Sometimes, the worry was not only *in* fiction but *about* fiction. George Gissing's *New Grub Street* (1891) is a celebrated novel of the uncelebrated, a story of how commitment and integrity are no guarantees of success in the writer's life. Edward Reardon, one of

---

[17]George Combe, *Elements of Phrenology*, 3rd edn (Edinburgh: Anderson, 1828), pp. 55, 193.
[18]Rudyard Kipling, *The Light That Failed* (London: Macmillan, 1891), p. 87.

Gissing's main characters, is a writer and a great worrier. And he's terribly bothered that others will realize that his life isn't proving a success. "One of Reardon's minor worries at this time," Gissing's narrator remarks of his struggling novelist, "was the fear that by chance he might come upon a review of 'Margaret Home.'" This is Reardon's novel. The shock of coming across a bad opinion is awful in anticipation:

> Since the publication of his first book he had avoided as far as possible all knowledge of what the critics had to say about him; his nervous temperament could not bear the agitation of reading these remarks, which, however inept, define an author and his work to so many people incapable of judging for themselves.[19]

There is a sharp rebuke to the fiction critics here who can dent not only a man's reputation but his peace of mind. And there's also an acceptance of the tense state of "nerves," the bodily tremulousness critics induce. The shaking frame of a man with a "nervous temperament" is that which is beginning to describe the new worrier—and the trouble over the reviews is, Gissing dispiritingly says, only one of Reardon's *minor* worries.

Worry begins to seep into fictional representations of modern life—often associated with the new urban and suburban lives, the pressure of modern work. Worry, in turn, started to appear in the new genre of self-help books. An important starting point for this genre had been the mid-nineteenth-century conception of the *duty* of (often lower middle-class) individuals to improve: to educate themselves, to develop new knowledge, skills, and abilities, as part of their general responsibility as morally upright and financially prudent individuals. Samuel Smiles's *Self-Help* (1859) was a landmark of this

---

[19]George Gissing, *New Grub Street* (Harmondsworth: Penguin, 1985), p. 239.

often lower-middle class conviction. And Smiles's book bequeathed its name, unknowingly, to the modern form of manuals that were not so concerned with the *duty* of improvement but simply with the *advantages* of lifting the burden of failure and unhappiness from troubled human lives.

In the period after the First World War, these self-help manuals were flourishing. They were keen to help the busy reader deal with their problems. And as worry began to appear on the book shelves, it was ironically clear that it was here to stay. "*Chronic fear—worry,*" said William S. Sadler in *Worry and Nervousness or The Science of Self-Mastery* (1914), an early set of reflections on how to stop worrying, is "a purely psychic condition characterized by inability to relax the attention when it has once fastened itself on a given idea—usually a persistently entertained fear of some sort."[20] "Entertained" is a winningly odd word to use here. It's as if worry has been deliberately offered hospitality, an invitation to a shaky, nervous party where all the drinks get spilled.

Sadler thought worry, likely enough, was part of a sequence and that chronic worry was a step on the way to serious mental illness. Once you started fretting, you were on a greasy pole that had mental ruin at the bottom. That was, unless you were able to get a grip, to practice "the science of self-mastery." Here was a bracing outlook, though the idea that worry was always ready to lead to serious mental illness was, as I've said, to become commonplace. It is still a great temptation to believe, as if it is easier to place "worry" firmly among the catalog of established "mental health" issues rather than adopt a more difficult, demanding, and untidy conception of what constitutes "mental health." This slippage between worry and a pathological

---

[20]William S. Sadler, *Worry and Nervousness or The Science of Self-Mastery* (London: Cazenove, 1914), p. 5.

state encouraged many early authors on worry to write prose that was caught between the reassuring and the threatening; between the psychological and the theological.

Haydn Brown's *Worry, and How to Avoid It* (1900) was typical in suggesting that readers could "think themselves out" of worry before it became truly problematic. There was the dimmest echo of ancient Stoicism here. "The great Jenner," Brown said, remembering the smallpox vaccine pioneer, Edward Jenner (1749–1823):

> found that in some instances a slight form of disease prevented a more serious one, and he instituted vaccination for people who wished to avoid small-pox. Worry should be dealt with in much the same manner; an attenuated mental exercise should be induced, so that the troubled brain may be brought under its antidotal and beneficent influence.[21]

The brain could apply its own strength to its own weakness. But what exactly does that mean? There's a peculiar fusion, or confusion, of ideas here about what the "brain" might be. Brown's use of a vaccination metaphor half-suggests that the trouble with worry is somatic; that it actually relates to a material condition of the brain, as smallpox is a physiological, observable, material condition. The conception of an "attenuated mental exercise" deploys an adjective usually applied to physical things and hints again that such exercise is akin to developing something as solidly real as a muscle. And yet Brown is, still, talking about a "mental" or not merely or hardly at all physical realm.

Mental control of mental problems was the most familiar solution to this new condition that seemed to be settling down as a recognized state of mind on both sides of the Atlantic. In the United States, the

---

[21]Haydn Brown, *Worry, and How to Avoid It* (London: Bowden, 1900), p. 37.

physician George Lincoln Walton, in the encouragingly named *Why Worry?* (1908), considered training in self-control would take "the edge off our worry." Self-control would enable worriers "to react more comfortably to our surroundings, thus not only rendering us more desirable companions, but contributing directly to our own health and happiness."[22] Stoicism again. If we could get mentally on top of worry then, apart from anything else, we would have more friends. The tedium of listening to a worrier would be reduced. Trying to facilitate new ways of thinking as a method for dealing with mental anxiety, Walton set terms that are still present in psychotherapy and cognitive behavioral therapy. His assumption that irrational ways of thinking (that is, "worrying") could be countered and cured by a rational philosophy of life was a version of a great liberal hope for the "treatment" of worry by reason. His therapy was grounded in a firm faith that the mind was susceptible to the compelling power of logic and that, if we behaved reasonably, we wouldn't suffer.[23]

Sometimes self-control was combined with the theology of transgression. Worry, as a not-mental-health problem, could be defeated by an individual's commitment to God. The American "New Thought" disciple and author of a once-famous book, *He Can who Thinks He Can, and Other Papers on Success in Life* (1911), Orison Sweet Marden (1850–1924), thought that those who worried simply needed to trust more in divine goodness and divine guidance. "We live and move and have our being in Him," Marden declared in *The Conquest of Worry* (1924), quoting Acts 17:28. "If we give way to paltry fear," he went on, "we but disappoint the divine purpose."[24] Marden's conception of a personal God—he assumed that God knew

---

[22]George Lincoln Walton, *Why Worry?* (Philadelphia, PA: Lippincott, 1908), p. 13.
[23]This is discussed in John Richard Orens, "The First Rational Therapist: George Lincoln Walton and Mental Training," *Journal of Rational-Emotive Therapy*, 4 (1986), pp. 180–4.
[24]Orison Sweet Marden, *The Conquest of Worry* (London: Rider, 1924), p. 7.

and judged every individual's every thought and feeling—turns worry into a sin. To worry is to doubt a future that's in God's care. Worrying privileges a human being's understanding (or lack of it) about what is to come over the wisdom of an all-seeing omniscience who already knows.

This part of worry's history concerns the establishment by the early twentieth century of a label for a condition that, swiftly enough, needed little glossing. At this stage, a stigma around conceptions of worry remained, as if Joseph Worcester's admonishing finger was still there. In turn, the business of curing worry was not only individually helpful but touched with a moral or even explicitly Christian dignity. Other writers in the early twentieth century, however, didn't think only of the individual mind of the individual worrier. They saw that there was something larger than a single man or woman's problem and something different from that individual's relationship with God. These writers on worry looked to apply an antidote not to an individual but to—the new twentieth century. Worry was not only in the moment. It was of the moment. Worry belonged to a particular stage of human culture, here and now.

George Lincoln Walton said in 1908, decisively, that worry was "'the disease of the age.'"[25] He didn't mean, at this point, that it was the "disease" in which the age was most interested, which had a peculiar cultural visibility, or even peculiar fashionability. He meant that it was a "disease" produced by the age. That was, clearly enough, a suggestive anticipation of "bioculture." Walton, a neurologist at Harvard University Medical School and Massachusetts General Hospital, was, in fact, merely repeating the title of a larger study that had made that bold claim its main diagnosis of modern life. Caleb Williams Saleeby (1878–1940), a prolific author on medical matters

---

[25]Walton, *Why Worry?* p. 17.

and an early student of genetics, found worry startlingly and almost embarrassingly a clue to the present day in his frankly titled book, *Worry the Disease of the Age*. This study, published in 1907, went into successive editions, plainly catching something of the *Zeitgeist*. The contemporary time might be, Saleeby said, "the greatest [age] in human history hitherto."[26] But it was be-devilled by worriers.

The swirl of modern British and American urban life was the culprit. Men and women were living with too many demands, not enough time, and too many expectations. They were living in cities that were too crowded, too fast, too-rapidly growing, and in which change was happening all the time. Life was overflowing with opportunities to fret. Time was newly valuable: time was money. Even *getting* to work on time involved negotiating with trains and buses and trams, with the new level of modern life's timetabling. Everywhere in the working day were demands and ticking clocks. Competitiveness was the defining word of new city life. And competitiveness was exhausting. Sadler considered that another word for worry could simply be "'Americanitis,' or the High Pressure Life."[27] Saleeby thought that worry was peculiarly the problem not only of busy, high-pressured nations, but of advanced ones that used their brains too much. The Spanish, the Greeks, and the Italians do not suffer from worry, Saleeby unblushingly said, as they are too idle and don't think very vigorously. But England and the United States are much further up the evolutionary chain and their people are living on their wits all the time. No wonder they worry.

Such provocative assertions aside, the notion of the modern city as the place where worry bred was becoming too plausible a claim to dismiss. High pressure was both powerful and deadly: new machinery

---

[26]C. W. Saleeby, *Worry the Disease of the Age* (Cambridge, MA: Smith, 1907), p. 1.
[27]The title of Chapter 9.

might produce force to multiply yield and increase efficiency. Yet force was that which, building in the head, brought strokes and paralysis. But if worry was from high pressure, it was also associated with low pressure, the running out of energy, with flagging and enervation. Through worry life drained. With worry, life passed in a fuzz of anxiety that was not productive but destructive. So it certainly seemed to the British poet W. H. Auden (1907–73) in his short poem "As I walked out one evening" (November 1937). That envisaged how worry was part of the state of being modern—and weary of it. Worry defined what we were, or could easily become, when life was frittered away in dissatisfactions and minor irritants, in the exhausting business of not having enough to keep us eager and keen. "In headaches and in worry," Auden wrote, "Vaguely life leaks away."[28] They're lines that make me think two things at once. First, "Ah yes, how true that is; how well Auden recognizes what so much of ordinary life is like." At the same time, I also think: "NO! I *must not* let my life become like this: I must live like to the full!" Auden's words have a seductive power to make me believe, and then reject, the idea that worry itself is something I can almost relax into and thus relieve myself of the responsibility of doing anything more strenuous or successful with life. A headache, after all, is a well-known way of avoiding all sorts of things. As a companion of misty "Vagueness," Auden's lines for a moment tease me with the notion that worry might be something of a vacation.

It's a dark realization that worry had become well established in the West after the First World War. The anxious waiting for a knock on the door, a telegram, a visit from an army officer or chaplain, brought worry into homes with horrible frequency. The enforced lack of knowledge, the uncertainty of what was happening at the Front,

---

[28]W. H. Auden, *Collected Poems*, ed. Edward Mendelson (London: Faber, 2007), p. 134.

the peril of communication, the danger and destruction—in such conditions, worry couldn't fail to flourish. And that's to say nothing of the worrying soldiers who were actually fighting. No wonder one of the most famous of First World War marching songs, "Pack up your troubles" (1915), included the memorable chorus:

> Pack up your troubles in your old kit-bag,
> And smile, smile, smile,
> While you've a lucifer to light your fag,
> Smile, boys, that's the style.
> What's the use of worrying?
> It never was worth while, so
> Pack up your troubles in your old kit-bag,
> And smile, smile, smile.[29]

Obviously enough, this is a version of Marden's conviction that a positive outlook on life will defeat baseless worries. Only here, at war, worry was hardly baseless. Only here, there may not have been much *use* for worrying but there was an astonishing amount to worry about.

Away from the trenches, was there something just a little *alluring* about worry? Perhaps there was the faint hint of the glamorous on the edge of those early twentieth-century claims that worry was the peculiar product of contemporary urban living, of the "High Pressure" life, of being modern. When London's Palace Theatre in 1913, just before the First World War, put on an entertainment titled, *I Should Worry*, it was a small effort to see, more plainly, if the new condition had any literal fashionability that might interest a paying audience. There is "a season for everything," said *The Times* reviewer

---

[29]The lyrics and music were by George and Felix Powell, and the song was published by Chappell in London in 1915.

the morning after watching it and there was "every sign last night that the season for *I Should Worry* has come."[30] She or he meant in terms of London taste. But, almost comically, the words inscribed the visibility of worry as something that was fashionable, almost "in season," too.

There's nothing glamorous in worry born of war. Yet part of the early history of worrying in the twentieth century concerns its appearance in art that had pleasure, fashionability, and modernity as part of its aim. The last part of this "short" history of worry— everyday worry's emergence into the language of the everyday—is worry's arrival more amply in literary language that probed imagined versions of sophisticated consciousnesses. Worry had appeared sketchily in realist fiction at the end of the nineteenth century. But in fiction of the early decades of the twentieth, including in specifically Modernist writing, worry was envisaged more fully from the inside. It was peculiarly seen, I think, through inner monologues that laid open a seductive version of private minds. Alongside the self-help books and experience of war, alongside the dictionary definitions and the alleged cures, worry was creeping into the high end of creativity.

For word art—poetry, drama, fiction—there was, as there still is, a problem in putting worry fully into words. It's a difficult problem to solve. Worry's hard to make interesting. It can be remorselessly uninteresting. Worry has had a long courtship with tedium. It has little visual presence and so the new cinema of the early twentieth century was not, so far as I can tell, its natural home. Worry's patterns are not obviously dramatic but, usually, tiresomely circular. There aren't necessarily great moments of revelation, of *anagnorisis*; there aren't sudden scenes of dramatic change, discovery, or redemption. Worry, said Sadler, "is seldom likely to cure itself by being allowed to

---

[30]*The Times*, Tuesday, August 12, 1913; p. 13; Issue 40288; column D. I do not know if this entertainment was built around L. Wolfe Gilbert's brief score *I Should Worry* (New York: Harry Von Tilzer Music Publishing, 1911).

run its natural course." And its natural course is almost always back on itself. "[Worrying] soon wears for itself definite grooves in the brain and nervous system," he went on, and "ever tends to perpetuate itself after the manner of [a] 'vicious circle,' and in almost every case slowly but surely increases its intensity, thereby becoming more and more destructive to mental peace and physical health."[31] Destructive to peace and in turn resistant to an engaging plot, worry, going around in its vicious circles, doesn't seem like an obvious topic for imaginative writers looking for something readable. Yet the strangest topics can make for interesting stories, given the right circumstances. What's strangest about the place of this potentially tedious subject in the early twentieth century is that Modernists took it up because, paradoxically, worry suggested to them the very sensitivity, even the troubled humanity, of some of its most interesting figures.

Worry was certainly a *theme* and a matter for *representation*. Undeniably, modern characters at the beginning of the twentieth century were suffering from worry even if they were not specifically Modern*ist*. Ralph Kent Buckland's short fiction, simply titled *Worry* (1914), was a brave American picture of a woman who worries; a venturesome exploration of the newly labeled form of mental pain. "Mrs. Simkins [. . .] sat poised regardless, cogitating, very much absorbed," Buckland wrote about his chief worrier, dismayed about the state of her furniture. She was:

deep in the mental gymnastics which have taken unto themselves among Americans as a class the name "worry." With the backward swing of the chair she paused, perilously poised, her weight on the tips of the rockers, her balance maintained by the hassock upon which her generous sized feet rested. She stopped a moment in her

---

[31]Sadler, *Worry and Nervousness*, pp. 65–6.

even back and forth, hesitating as though the better to assimilate a hazy or but half grasped portion of what was on her mind.

Sufficient evidence there lay down in the front cellar under the parlor (for though the house was small, its cellar was walled off into rooms) of the risks to be chanced in attempting thus to interrupt the steady swing of a chair, in trying thus to pervert the long well-understood functions of the rocker; there in that front cellar, a crippled article of ease, lay John's favorite chair, a relic of their first days of housekeeping, one of the long curved rockers broken squarely off close to the frame. There doubtless it would lie for some time to come ere it could be restored to its erstwhile usefulness and beauty. Certain monetary annoyances obsessed the family, the repairing of broken pieces of furniture could not be planned for even for a moment.[32]

Mrs Simkins's anxiety about "certain monetary annoyances"—that's a nice way of putting it—gather around the furniture and the backward and forward motion of that rocking chair is a good emblem of the rocking of Mrs Simkins's mind through its cares. There's energy but not progress; effort but not advancement.

Worry blossomed into fiction on both sides of the Atlantic though, it's true, not often as a literal topic for a whole story. The English Modernist and feminist Virginia Woolf (1882–1941) was for a long time interested in "mental health." The collapse of her own led to her suicide in the River Ouse 2 years into the Second World War. There are deeply troubled individuals in her fiction, especially poor Septimus Warren Smith in *Mrs Dalloway* (1925). Traumatized by the First World War, he eventually kills himself too. But there are also the less troubled: the worriers. Woolf's characters include those whose inner lives are

---

[32]Ralph Kent Buckland, *Worry* (Boston, MA: Sherman, French, 1914), pp. 2–3.

fretful and her "inner monologue" technique of narration permits the reader the illusion of direct access to their minds. *To the Lighthouse* (1927) is one of the most widely read of Modernist works of fiction and it takes its reader deep into worrying as a troublesome companion of human interiority. Mr Ramsay's mind is no easy place to be. He's a half-recollection of Virginia Woolf's eminent father, Sir Leslie Stephen (1832–1904), who contributed his own depressing *Mausoleum Book* to the literature of acute mental suffering.[33] Mr Ramsay is a writer, a father, a husband, a self-absorbed individual, an academic—and a worrier. And he's particularly worried, like Gissing's hero, about his books. This certainly *is* worry: a set of nagging questions that won't go away, caught like flies buzzing inside Woolf's prose.

Mrs Ramsay, the patient, compassionate, large-minded wife of the worrying author, reflects on his inner state. Mr Ramsay, she observes,

> was always uneasy about himself. That troubled her. He would always be worrying about his own books—will they be read, are they good, why aren't they better, what do people think of me? Not liking to think of him so, and wondering if they had guessed at dinner why he suddenly became irritable when they talked about fame and books lasting, wondering if the children were laughing at that, she twitched the stockings out, and all the fine gravings came drawn with steel instruments about her lips and forehead, and she grew still like a tree which has been tossing and quivering and now, when the breeze falls, settles, leaf by leaf, into quiet.[34]

There is recognition, sympathy, and irritation. Worry's perilous to others, this passage half-admits: Mr Ramsay troubles his wife even as

---

[33] See *Sir Leslie Stephen's Mausoleum Book*, ed. by Alan Bell (Oxford: Clarendon, 1977).
[34] Virginia Woolf, *To the Lighthouse* (London: Vintage, 2004), p. 110.

he is troubled himself. Actually, he does more than trouble his wife. His anxieties form the broken center of his family, causing damage that Mrs Ramsay endeavors to repair. In the novel as a whole Mr Ramsay is at once pitiable and self-indulgent, suffering and vain. In this moment, nevertheless, Woolf's interested in a woman's consciousness of her husband's sensitivity, of his worrying about himself. A worrier is always, however awkwardly, deserving of *some* sympathy.

If Virginia Woolf represented worry, the Irish Modernist James Joyce (1882–1941) made the reader, I think, behave like a worrier. Joyce encouraged a kind of worried reading where we're invited to *worry at* the meaning of words. We're asked to see that there are underground anxieties weaving their way beneath the surface of the language, anxieties that are visible in *double entendres*, puns, ambiguities. *Ulysses* (1922) has a reputation for difficulty. But, if it *is* difficult, it's also familiar. Joyce's novel makes a great epic of modern life not, like Homer's, from heroes and Gods but from ordinary things. The novel is startlingly, overflowingly, full of the everyday, the immediately recognizable, the plain and the popular. And the reach of *Ulysses* into the ordinary world of 1904 (when it is set) includes dealing with the disease of the age.

Ulysses is the story of one man, Leopold Bloom, walking around Dublin on June 16, 1904. He's a new kind of Odysseus and the episodes in his day are new versions of Homer's hero's adventures. (It's worth pointing out, to be scrupulous, that Joyce didn't want his readers to become *too* obsessed by the Greek parallels and removed the chapter headings that had once drawn attention to them.) The scope of the novel is minute and obsessional, but it is also enormous—about Great Britain and Ireland; the experience and meaning of exile; about European culture; the place of myth in modern life; about the modern novel and what it can do; about the Victorians; about human memory and the inner life; about the limits of realism; about the relationship between language and thought; about the nature of morals; about sex. Yet *Ulysses* is also the story of a worried man. Mr Bloom frets. And he worries, not least, a bit like his mythic Greek predecessor, about what's happening back at home. Is Bloom's wife, Molly, unfaithful or about to be unfaithful? What has happened to Mr Bloom's marriage?

Molly is "in the pink," Bloom says, "gaily," to a minor character, Mrs Breen, before immediately changing the subject.[35] But Molly's situation is more than merely "in the pink" for her husband and he finds it impossible, underneath, to change the subject at all. The vocabulary of sexual worry creeps slowly into the language circulating around Bloom. It won't go away. In the so-called Lotus Eaters episode (to use one of the headings Joyce didn't like), Bloom "unrolled the newspaper baton idly and read idly," seeing the memorable advertisement:

> *What is home without*
> *Plumtree's Potted Meat?*
> *Incomplete.*
> *With it an abode of bliss.*

Then his conversation with M'Coy, another minor character, continues:

—My missus has just got an engagement. At least it's not settled yet.

Valise tack again. By the way no harm. I'm off that, thanks.

Mr. Bloom turned his largelidded eyes with unhasty friendliness.

—My wife too, he said. She's going to sing at a swagger affair in the Ulster Hall, Belfast, on the twenty-fifth.

—That so? M'Coy said. Glad to hear that, old man. Who's getting it up?

---

[35] *U*, 8:205. All references are to James Joyce, *Ulysses: The Corrected Text*, student edition, ed. Hans Walter Gabler with Wolfhard Steppe and Claus Melchior (Harmondsworth: Penguin, 1986) and are given in the standard form using "*U*."

Mrs. Marion Bloom. Not up yet. Queen was in her bedroom eating bread and. No book. Blackened court cards laid along her thigh by sevens. Dark lady and fair man. Letter. Cat furry black ball. Torn strip of envelope.

> *Love's*
> *Old*
> *Sweet*
> *Song*
> *Comes lo-ove's old . . .*

—It's a kind of a tour, don't you see, Mr. Bloom said thoughtfully. *Sweeeet song.* There's a committee formed. Part shares and part profits. (*U*, 5:143–63)

The language, symptomatically, is caught between the mundane, the vulgar, and the revelatory. It pulls the reader back to Bloom's underlying worry. What's significant here is that the reader is able to read for *signs* of worry in the dialogue and the narration of inner thoughts. The patterns of allusions and references work not only in the service of the passage's coherence but are the stubborn marks of fretfulness, of something that vexes persistently.

The Plumtree's advertisement describes home as "an abode of bliss." How ironic! And that thought is, appropriately, quickly disturbed by Bloom's "it's not settled yet," which is at once true of Molly's singing engagement and, alas, of the Blooms's domestic life, unsettled by her lover, Blazes Boylan. Dimly, the "swagger affair" echoes with that sexual affair too and the awkward phrasing of "Who's getting it up?" refers—we can hardly avoid noticing—not only to the organizer of the Ulster Hall event but to Boylan, Molly's would-be sexual partner. With a shifted question mark, the words track the uncomfortable sexual narrative worrying Bloom: "Who's getting it up

[. . .] Mrs. Marion Bloom?" The reply, as the prose winds on—"Not up yet"—is awkwardly, awfully, true of Boylan's nearly begun affair. Even that final "part shares [. . .] part profits" distractingly alludes to Molly as a time-share sexual partner too, confirming Bloom's inability to shed his worry, to forget his marital anxieties.

Ulysses is a remarkable story about a worried man partly because it lets the reader into exchanges like this. Joyce allows us to worry at the words—like "getting it up"—and then to realize that Bloom's worries are visible through them, as if they have spilled into and tainted the language around him. Bloom's day is a circle. He sets out from his house, 7 Eccles Street, at the beginning of the novel and returns there, in the "Ithaca" episode, at the end. He enacts, physically, the course of his worry—literally moving away from Molly and returning to her (though not to sleep with her). *Ulysses* encourages a reader to understand, to *feel*, how a worry lurks under words and keeps pulling meaning back to an underlying issue. And it's worry-shaped in its very plotting of a journey away from, then back to, the source of the trouble.

This literature wasn't widely read. It'd be a mistake to think that *To the Lighthouse* and *Ulysses* were for mass consumption and they remain, by and large, at the top end of reading tastes. Such texts, perhaps, can't be satisfactorily used to reveal anything too grand about a whole culture. But these magnificent novels of High Modernism say important things about worry, nevertheless, for they're still part of the library of words that structure how and what is thought, how and in what ways we have understood and described ourselves in different class, gender, historical, and cultural locations. "Worry," a concept with a label, comes prominently into the English language at the beginning of the twentieth century. And so, in turn, it appears in some of the most arresting, demanding, and moving literature of its time. That's hardly a surprise. Such literature records the word's spread just as it helped to make worry known, and, even, vicariously experience-able. Imaginative writing prepares readers; it grooms them. Quietly, such writing shapes what readers expect from life and from consciousness, eloquently providing us with a language to envisage ourselves *to* ourselves and to others. The appearance of the worrier in early twentieth-century literature as a woman- or man-of-the-moment, a particular kind of modern person, was not merely a perceptive observation of how things were between the two World Wars. It was a way of shaping expectations about what, exactly, being human was now like.

Worry's appearance in the early twentieth century marks its "emergence into discourse," its availability as a concept in the language of human analysis and self-knowledge. That's the "short" or "local" history of worry. It's the not-very-far-back-story. And it would be correct to say that worry has never gone away. As a noun and, more importantly, as a state of mind with which men and women remain familiar, worry has become part of the air we now breathe, or, as Henry James would beautifully put it, part of the light by which we walk. Who'd really need to be told in English-speaking countries of the West what "worry" now was?

But something else has occurred.

If worry firmly established itself in language between the two World Wars, what, exactly, happened to it? The self-help books and the novel writers found a place for worrying after the First World War. The novelists, particularly, developed vocabularies in which worry could be spoken about, represented, dramatized, and even passed on. But it'd be wrong to think that worry became a subject for which there's a sophisticated critical vocabulary, an extensive literature, a range of theories, a choice of interpretations, a sequence of schools of thought. For all the creative legacy of the Modernists and the largely forgotten body of early self-help books, worry hasn't established itself as a topic for detailed study, for much thoughtful writing, for extensive representation and discussion, or for much consideration at all except in the *new* self-help books that promise peace of mind. (It would be tempting, and convenient, to think that phrase "peace of mind" was a relatively new one but in fact *OED* dates to 1583.)

Worry's still experienced more than it's analyzed; it's still lived more than examined. To think about worry now is to be an investigator of the known-yet-almost-unknown, of the paradoxically familiar but almost undiscussed. To think about worry is to look beneath often polished surfaces and probe layers of camouflage. It's to undertake a mission to recover the histories of ordinary mental pain that aren't lost but occluded; of which we aren't ignorant but shy.

2

O day and night, but this is wondrous strange!

Hamlet, 1:5:166

I just said that writing about worry could now be conceived, in part, as a "mission." That's rather a grand, even grandiose, way of putting it. It's certainly provocative and it may be unwise. I am definitely giving my task a noble label, one that might seem pretentious. In recovering the "hidden histories of ordinary pain," there is, to be sure, always the possibility of something dignified and humane. Here's a task of freeing up, and making visible, stories of trouble and discomfort that are usually submerged. Doing that is surely no ignoble undertaking? There's some credit in it. Recognizing pain, and allowing it to be talked about, may help restore confidence and self-worth to sufferers who will recognize themselves part of a community and, perhaps, supported, understood.

But there's another side to worry. The side that makes us relieved it's *not* talked about.

There's a local and a broader point to make about this relief. Here's the local one. A friend of mine knows well why worry might better not be talked about. Her story is symptomatic even as it is, at the same time, extreme. For 2 or even 3 years, from when she was about 16, Ruth faced quite serious worry almost every day—and it wasn't her own. Indeed, this was worry—as she looks back at it now—which was close to a clinically recognizable anxiety disorder. Sensible and caring, even though young, Ruth possessed the double-edged quality of being "easy to talk to." People enjoyed speaking to her because, even as a young woman, she was, I understand, sympathetic. Ruth was good at asking the right questions and good—at the right moments—at not asking them. As a consequence, she was frequently squeezed out of conversations by others' needs, stories, views, and feelings. She was readily silenced by the emotional demands of other people. The problem was that, because she was so "easy to talk to," others thought she didn't mind listening to them—pretty much all the time. Being "easy to talk to" can bring out the worst in people.

I didn't know her then. What I know now was that Ruth lived with what she thought of as her "worry sister." I know now that almost every evening, when she had taken the bus home from school, she was faced by the emotional demands of someone who absorbed reassurance without being reassured. Her elder sister's worries were legion. But they were usually focused one at a time, on a sequence of single issues that included, for instance, failure, insecurity, future poverty, being boring, being fat, being unattractive, being stupid, being unpopular, or occasionally being ill. There Ruth's sister would be, sitting on the sofa in front of the gas fire when my friend returned home, and she'd run through in enormous fretful detail what was wrong this time. The crack and snap of an old-fashioned gas fire expanding and contracting in the heat became a peculiarly uncomfortable sound for Ruth. What was wrong was almost always different from what had been wrong the week before and sometimes even the day before. There were times when the worry lifted and there were many more times when it changed. But for the most part, Ruth stayed, she tells me now, almost every evening to listen to the worries of a sister whom she loved but who was, as she half-knew, asking for emotional support Ruth could only give at a cost and which hardly seemed to be support at all.

The first costs were frustration and loss of time. Ruth would assure her sister that the faint dizziness she felt at work couldn't be serious because she didn't have other troubling symptoms. She had no pins-and-needles, no blinding headaches, no serious loss of balance, no hint of sight deterioration. She was eating well and looked fit enough. But the following day, Ruth's sister would either be back where she started or facing a new problem, a new circular worry. This—and it's an extreme case, I know—was emptying a pool with a leaking limpet shell. My friend was back where she started. Reassurance, knowledge, advice, sympathy—there seemed to be nothing decisively able to shift Ruth's sister for long from her fixed belief that there was, today, something risky about tomorrow. More often than not, the conversations only ended when someone else came in, or the phone rang, or the dinner needed seeing to. Something random, almost absurdly ordinary, worked better than the frustrated kindness of a very young woman. The conversations, the near-monologues, were abandoned or interrupted. They weren't concluded.

The expense of my friend's spirit on this neediness and suffering was frustrating as she now recognizes. This was labor in which Ruth couldn't progress; work without issue; comfort without comforting. My friend wanted to help but she could not. Daily tranquility was lost and Ruth experienced reluctance at going home, a sorrow for her sister and her apparent helplessness, and a half-anger that her own life seemed to be ignored. One person's worries were all there was in that front room. The longer term cost was, as Ruth would say herself now, damage to her expectations of what human relationships were and, more particularly, family life was like. That damage, at least as she thinks of it today, was enduring. In the abstract, Ruth can imagine a happy, mutually supportive, and "give-and-take" family life for herself. But she can't quite believe in it. It's a theoretical not a living idea. She finds it hard to shake off the inner intuition, her inner faith, that any future family of her own could not be happy. Her sister's sadly endless appetite for reassurance has left her with the felt certainty that families are no place for her.

The early self-help books were candid about worry as something that made the worrier difficult to get on with. And the situation didn't have to be anywhere near as extreme as Ruth's. Worrying can be a form of vanity. It can be a species of self-indulgence, a way of extending ego into a conversation, or of somehow confirming *selfness* in the head. To worry silently is to feel a certain kind of closeness to oneself, to the "real" needy person that one may believe oneself to be. To *talk* to others about worries is, in some ways, always to declare: look at me; listen to *my* pains; listen to what *I* live with; *I* am important in my own worry. This is to make of one's own inner thoughts the substance of conversations with others so that conversations cease and monologues take over. Sometimes, even my best friends drink a good deal more than they should as they sit in pubs listening wearily to Me and My Woes. Sometimes the idea of having a busy inner life is a pain in the backside for other people.

There's a peculiar form of comfort in worry for the worrier. Maybe that's why Buckland associated it with a rocking chair. When worry is the familiar state of mind, it's hard to give up because it is a risk to try life without it. Returning to worry, under those circumstances, is like an odd home-coming; counterintuitively, it's to recover safety— however bizarre the worrier may know that, at some level, this all to be. Worry can seem so much part of a worrier that we almost confuse ourselves for worry—as T. S. Eliot joined his name and the sound of worrying as if they were the same thing. To worry is, in this sense, to express a perceived essence of the self, the self that seems most real to the worrier. And that, in the midst of a search for reassurance, is faintly—reassuring.

There're good reasons why worry might be best kept private. Hidden histories of pain can be hidden expressions of self-centeredness. And those, more often than not, are better repressed.[1] Maybe there is something valuable in that old notion of self-control after all. There can't be much noble in encouraging these narratives of inner fretfulness to be made more visible, more recognizable. Some of the early self-help books were abrasive, but sometimes persuasive, in confronting such indulgence. "It will not do," said the anonymous author of *Don't Worry* (1900) firmly, "To let ourselves slide [. . .] We must fight the Natural Tendency of Worry. We must resist Worry: not its coming (it is sure to come), but what it tends to make us when it comes."[2] The implication that the worrier is a nuisance still resonates—sometimes with toe-curling clarity. A worrier can easily seem like a baby bird—mouth open; calling attention to itself; focused only on what others can do for it. In *To the Lighthouse*, Virginia Woolf had a penetrating portrait of this side of a man of worry. Mr Ramsay, at his most unsympathetic, is the opposite of a lighthouse. He doesn't give out energy for the benefit of others. He absorbs energy at others' cost.

---

[1] For an unforgettable account of a memory that could not be repressed, see Patricia van Tighem, *The Bear's Embrace: A True Story of Surviving a Grizzly Bear Attack* (Vancouver: Greystone, 2000). The role of memory and repression in recovering from near-death experiences was discussed stimulatingly in http://www.theguardian.com/lifeandstyle/2012/nov/09/life-after-near-death (last accessed January 30, 2014).

[2] [Anonymous], *Don't Worry*, by the author of *A Country Parson* (New York: Caldwell, 1900?), pp. 13, 15.

Mr Ramsay's son is trying to read but there is his father, vampirically drawing in the vital powers of everyone present. Mr Ramsay deserved some pity, Woolf's narrator says:

> But his son hated him. He hated him for coming up to them, for stopping and looking down on them; he hated him for interrupting them; he hated him for the exaltation and sublimity of his gestures; for the magnificence of his head; for his exactingness and egotism (for there he stood, commanding them to attend to him); but most of all he hated the twang and twitter of his father's emotion which, vibrating round them, disturbed the perfect simplicity and good sense of his relations with his mother. By looking fixedly at the page, he hoped to make him move on; by pointing his finger at a word, he hoped to recall his mother's attention, which, he knew angrily, wavered instantly his father stopped. But, no. Nothing would make Mr. Ramsay move on. There he stood, demanding sympathy.[3]

Mr Ramsay has little time for his son. His own needs are, at this moment, all that he can recognize. How that phrase, the "twang and twitter of his [. . .] emotion," haunts me—and no doubt my hungover friends. But an even worse version of the egotistical worrier occurs when the worrier, often a close family member, *does* have time, too much time, for their family and friends. The even more difficult version of Mr Ramsay is the worrier who mistakes worry—for love.

How easily the worrier finds that love can be about the self! The worrier's mental habits make us peculiarly susceptible to this failing. Here, it may seem, is another kind of worry that's best hidden, best repressed, best not talked about. This is worry that shouldn't be brought into the open as part of a noble-sounding but ill-conceived attempt to

---

[3]Woolf, *To the Lighthouse*, p. 34.

release "hidden histories of pain." Mature, grown-up love is, at least in part, about two people. It's true that the gloomy English novelist Thomas Hardy (1840–1928) couldn't see this, even in his earlier more buoyant fiction. "The rarest offerings of the purest loves," he said sourly in *Far from the Madding Crowd* (1874), "are but a self-indulgence, and no generosity at all."[4] But, well, not everyone sees it like that.

Love that works well, whatever else it is, requires *some* recognition of another's difference, another's (semi-)independent being. Two people don't become one when they fall in love with each other. They don't become one when they marry, despite the words of Genesis 2:24. They need, always, to know the other's not-one-ness, their closeness but also their difference. Worry, however, as I'm thinking about it here, is an easier kind of "love." It's easier *than* love. Worry substitutes that difficult recognition of another's separateness with the demands of the self. Worry enables love to become, with sometimes horrible visibility, the extension of neediness. The worrier who mistakes worry for love is someone who, characteristically, frets about another's safety, or health, or job security *too much*. The fretting is more conspicuous than anything. This is a familiar kind of familial love but it isn't only familial. Here, worry's no doubt born from a particularly intense breed of insecurity manifested in fearfulness about letting go; from a difficulty with recognizing dissimilarity; from a more general human problem about knowing what to do with Someone Who is Not Me.

How many tales of vexation, I wonder, start here? The parent who needs to know that their son has got home safely after a visit and can't relax until they hear he has, may be genuinely caring, genuinely wanting the safety of their child. But they may be thinking more about themselves and their own needs. Love doesn't put itself forward in this way and compete for emotional visibility. Love thinks of others

---

[4]Thomas Hardy, *Far from the Madding Crowd*, 2 vols (London: Smith Elder, 1874), i.217.

and worrying about them is not the same thing. The boyfriend who can't stop phoning his girlfriend to make sure she is okay or the husband who can't sleep until his wife is back from a night out may be genuinely caring, genuinely wanting the safety of their partners. But they may be thinking about themselves most, using their worries as a way of putting themselves at the center of the emotional dynamics. There's a hard truth here. There's something easy about worry and something egotistic.

For all those who hustle love out with fretfulness, there's a similar sense of what constitutes success and happiness, a similar sense of what makes a successful family life. It's defined by a simple negative. Happiness exists in the state of not being worried.

"Feeling okay" is determined by an absence—a lack of pain or mental anxiety—and not by a rewarding presence of something affirming or pleasurable. And this is not, of course, only for those who make the worry/love confusion. It's true of worriers generally. Perhaps you can identify worriers by the way in which they answer a normal, casual inquiry about how they are. "Hi—are you OK?" "Hello!—how are things with you?" There are tell-tale answers. A worrier might be lurking behind the response: "Not too bad, thanks very much." Not *too* bad? The measure is the relative absence of gloominess, difficulty, problems, pain. Daring to be happy is a risk. It's easier for the worrier to define contentment in negative terms as the absence of much to be concerned about because it saves us from the audacity of trying out a new feeling. Yet even having an unusually small amount to worry about can be disturbing, a tidy way back to worrying. Being not *too* bad can quickly become Quite Bad Again. In Roger Hargreaves marvellous children's book *Mr. Worry* (1978), the hero, Mr Worry, has all his worries removed by a wizard. Shortly afterward, he starts to worry about having nothing to worry about. That's about right, I'd say.

But then there's still the broader problem of why we mightn't want to talk too much about worry. This is a fault line throughout this book and I keep tripping over it. There's contradiction. I want at once to attend to worriers and put worry into language so that we can admit it and talk about it. I also want to be faithful to an anxiety that talking about worry is egotistical and dull. Ruth's sister was a local if acute instance of an ampler, looser moral problem. How much attention should we demand for ourselves and the facts of our own individuality, the minuteness of our own experience of the world, the pulses and flickers of our conscious life? Indeed, what kind of "right" do we have to make ourselves and our own problems so well-aired anyway? Where does that "right" come from? And, beyond that, what "responsibilities" has anyone got to listen to us or to do anything about what we say? There's some danger that my book contributes to the development of some pretty antisocial attitudes.

I can't easily make up my mind between sympathy and judgment. I'm caught between welcoming the language of worry and being irritated by my own subject. At one level, I'd like to be able to live in a community where it's possible to talk about the little or larger pains of the inner life. And, at another, I have a dreadful feeling that this is self-centered and in conflict with the necessities of a genuine community, in conflict with decent working relationships of give-and-take between human beings. I also fear, wholly hypocritically, having to listen too much to *others'* worries. "Don't think I am sympathetic," I often say to myself when someone starts telling me about their problems. "Apart from anything else, you're getting in the way of me talking about me."

Still, I can't avoid trying to find a way of delving further into the nature of human individuality by working on a language to speak of worries, to open up the secret landscapes of the worrier's mind. It is, after all, folly not to deal with human beings as they really are rather than as I'd like them to be. And worry, with its hidden histories of pain, invites some sorrow and asks for some understanding, whatever else it does. Despite all Mr Ramsay's unsympathetic demands for sympathy, he actually is in trouble. For all the fact that Ruth's sister was a nuisance, she really was having a tough time. It'd hardly be useful merely to claim that worriers should be dealt moral opprobrium, the reprimands of the early self-help books, the stern declarations that they are nothing but vain, egotistic, selfish. Whether I like it or not, I have to accept the existence of worry even though I know it can be vain, egotistic, selfish. I have to deal with worriers, not deny them.

All the anxiety that lies beneath the surface of everyday conversations, almost never heard, but always there: no wonder there's a commercial interest in trying to sort things out, to reduce, or even "cure" worry. Worry's true extent may be unknown, an occluded history of mental suffering. But something of the suffering, the sound of the squirrel's heartbeat, registers. And, apart from anything else, there is some money to be made from it. Ordinary worries are hardly spoken about in public. So it is no surprise that the center of worry therapy is in books. They can be read in private. They can be hidden away when the neighbors come round. Perhaps there's some apparent discordance with my theme in considering the contemporary self-help books, for they are almost always written by professional psychologists or practicing clinicians. Such books are usually based on accounts of worriers who have indeed sought professional medical or psychological help. Those are different from most of the worriers that I'm thinking about. Yet the readership of the self-help books is intended to include, exactly, the ordinary worrier. Those books are pitched at people who, probably, don't realize that they can be "cured" until they notice a book on curing worry in the shop or in an advertisement. You can be healed of worry, the books announce. However low level your worries are, we can fix them. That's a tempting proposal. I wonder, by the way, how many people buy worry self-help books for themselves and how many are bought *for others*. Are they ever given as presents?

"Hey, wow—*thanks a lot.*"

The self-help books of the early twentieth century are not entirely remote from their current descendents just as the early twentieth century's descriptions of worry aren't wholly redundant now. What was once an encouragement to think differently about worry after the First World War and so relieve the mind from its own pressures has now a formal label: cognitive behavioral therapy (CBT). This is about changing the script by which we live, making us aware that we *have* a script and that we can alter it (the notion that we have a script, learned in childhood as a survival technique, is a key part of Eric Berne's concept of Transactional Analysis, a widely used form of therapy for those with serious anxiety disorders).[5] CBT is a staple of the contemporary campaigns against problematic, disabling forms of worry, as for many other things. The self-help books suggest that, for better or for worse, even the secrets of our private selves can belong with those who "cure." The books affirm their authors, prominently, as the new sages, the new priests who know the secrets of our minds and can help us remedy what are coded as our "problems." Here are the secular world's new confessionals.

The anonymous author of *Conquering Fear and Worry* (c.1938), part of a British series encouragingly called *Live Successfully!*, was not untypical of what would become the modern genre. This brief book, with its reassuring exclamation mark, was certain that worry could be frightened off by determination and action. "Fear goes," the anonymous author said, "as soon as you start to do something about it."[6] The author, whoever he or she was, encourages readers to trace

---

[5] Eric Berne's *Games People Play: The Psychology of Human Relationships* (1964) is still widely read. The International Transaction Society, which promotes his analytical tools, can be discovered through http://www.itaaworld.org/ (last accessed January 23, 2014).
[6] [Anonymous], *Conquering Fear and Worry, Live Successfully! Book Number 3* (London: Odhams, c. 1938), p. 8.

the *likelihood* of what they were worried about taking place. This book
advises a rational exploration of our fears for the future and hopes, in
turn, to control the brain with itself. How probable, really, is that we
left the back door open? How likely, truly, is that this pain is anything
to be concerned about? Looked at in the round, is Billie *really* likely
to think you mean x rather than y in that letter? Thinking differently
and believing differently: these aspirations remain the cornerstones
of the self-help genre now. "Other people cannot make us afraid," said
Orison Marden:

> They may do things that tend to make us afraid, but it is only when
> we permit our minds to take up such suggestions from without,
> that we can become a prey to fear. Nothing can act upon or affect
> us until it gets into our mind.[7]

There it is: permitting our minds to let a worry in. Marden's language
makes it clear that it's only the worrier himself or herself who can stop
"giving permission" and, accordingly, take the upper hand with worry.
Mental strength will keep mental weakness out.

William Sadler, proponent of "self-mastery" where worry was
concerned, encouraged his readers to replace negative thoughts with
positive ones. He asked them to exchange doubts for convictions,
anxieties for imagined surety. But this was only really successful
when it was joined with the replacement of thought by faith, the
substitution of fretful reasoning with an open and willing decision
to trust. "No amount of mental resolution and moral determination,"
Sadler remarks:

> in and of themselves, will be able to overthrow and cast out worry.
> Positive thinking is not only required in the battle against worry,

---

[7]Marden, *The Conquest of Worry*, p. 3.

but it is essential that our positive thinking shall also be opposite thinking. We must overcome worry with its opposite mental states; we must cultivate faith and trust. This is the one vital factor in the permanent cure of worry: replace the worry thought with an opposite thought which will occupy the mind and inspire the soul. Drive out fear-thought by exercising faith-thought. This is the substitute cure for worry; and when backed up by the strong resolution of a determined will this method will always be found effective.[8]

The chance of healing lies, for the worrier, in swapping one form of mental activity for another. We can't merely argue ourselves out of worry or let someone else try to do it for us. We have to change what we believe. We have of our own will to trust in a better self and a better future. We have to decide to be happy and then have faith in what we decided.

The terms of the old self-help books have been reinterpreted for a new generation. Of the best-selling contemporary self-help manuals on worry, Dr Robert L. Leahy's *The Worry Cure: Stop Worrying and Start Living* (2005) is among the most popular and it's not hard to see why. It's humane and considerate, generous and benign. It is hugely optimistic. *The Worry Cure* offers both an account of bad ways of dealing with worry and a set of techniques for managing or "curing" it, or at least tricking worry into taking up a less dominant position in our lives. Part of *The Worry Cure*'s bond with its predecessors is its confidence, again, that worriers can sort out their own problems by changing something of what happens in our minds through our minds' power. Using the mind to cure the mind: there's mental homeopathy here.

---

[8]Sadler, *Worry and Nervousness*, pp. 305–6.

What *not* to do is clear. Poor ways, bad "Examples of Safety Behaviors," include the following responses to a typical species of worry. The typical worry is, for instance, that "I'll make a fool of myself speaking to that group." Such a worry is characteristically followed, as Leahy sees it, by this kind of reaction from the worrier: "Over prepare, read notes, rehearse over and over, avoid looking at the audience, scan the audience for signs of rejection, don't pick up water glass because of fear of hands shaking."[9] These are nervous methods for dealing with nerves. And such behaviors create new objects for worry ("have I prepared *enough*?") and in turn amplify problems rather than solve them. Better ways, Leahy proposes, help take the worrier out of worry or worry out of the worrier.

Leahy doesn't mean that we should avoid preparing for a presentation. It's just that we should be in a position to do it without worry, as centered, calm, and optimistic individuals, with self-belief that is enabling. Leahy describes, often using a "cost-benefit" approach to worry, how a high level of self analysis is emotionally profitable for the worrier. What's needed is a real intellectual curiosity about the roots of our own problems and a capacity to look at things differently. He thinks we can, literally, analyze worries away. In academia, politics, or business, it is easy to think that *analyzing* a problem has made it disappear, when it has done nothing of the sort. But Leahy suggests that analyzing worry really will make it vanish. His case is built on the idea that we must find out what our core anxiety is. Once we have done so, we must identify ways of "acting against" it. With luck, we will find that "core anxiety," which will typically be some inhibiting belief about ourselves, and cast it out. In exposing the core problem, we will not, in Leahy's imaginings, be defeated. We will be on the way

---

[9]Robert L. Leahy, *The Worry Cure: Stop Worrying and Start Living* (London: Piaktus, 2005), p. 51.

to conquering the very roots of our problems. Know thyself—and be free from worry.

Encouraging his readers to "act against" their beliefs, Leahy argues the opposite of Marden. Leahy perceives worry as a *form of belief* (in something negative) that needs to be tackled by *thought*. It's the act of thinking that will reveal affirmative ideas and potential exits to worry. Thinking will give us new grounds for more enabling faith in ourselves. This is fundamentally personal analysis. It's about getting to grips with the contents of our minds and changing them. The pressure is on you and me, where worry is concerned, to solve our own troubles. We're responsible for ourselves. In economics or politics, that's a crucial plank in the ideology of the free market. Here it is fundamental, apparently, to being happy.

Consider Darlene. She, according, to Dr Leahy, worried she was boring. She *believed* she was boring. "When she feels anxious," he says, "[Darlene] acts in a boring way. She avoids eye contact, puts a dumb smile on her face, and answers with one-word responses. When she is comfortable and knows that she can trust you, she is easy to talk to, has opinions, seems relaxed, and says interesting things."[10] But in the counseling session, Dr Leahy tried to encourage Darlene to challenge her apparently fixed belief that she was "fundamentally boring." This is similar to Berne's conception of changing the script. Dr Leahy's encouragement was to act against that fixed belief, to prove that it wasn't fixed after all. First, Leahy writes that he asked Darlene to initiate conversations with people she did not know by pretending that she was an interviewer. "Since the majority of people think that the most fascinating conversation is always about themselves," Leahy remarks with some acidity, "Darlene's job was to ask other people all about their interests and themselves, and then ask them more about

[10]Ibid., p. 163.

themselves."[11] With such an approach, Darlene had no responsibility to say anything about herself. The technique began to prove to her—despite the rather troubling grounds—that she could be popular. New people could find her appealing, even if, in fact, they were only enjoying the opportunities Darlene was providing them to forget she was there.

At this stage, Leahy is (almost) ready to admit that the mythological emblem of the worrier is the hydra. As soon as you cut off one head, there is at least one other in its place. Tackling one belief easily leads to another that requires attention. But the new (negative) beliefs can *also* be driven away with thought. And each time a new negative asserts itself, a better belief can be envisaged. Eventually, a constructive faith will emerge, a set of "more positive and more realistic belief[s]"[12] about oneself, which are robust and durable. This is the real achievement of healing, a glimpse of the therapist as the bringer of confidence, the hope of suffering men and women.

I admire this optimism. But I find it difficult to grasp the mental transactions going on when a therapist constructs the beliefs another should hold (however general and benign those beliefs are). Here is *argument* for *belief*—sometimes, indeed, merely assertions about what we should believe. The expectation of logical mental behavior, of sound reasoning, is a remarkable feature of how the self-help books think the self can be managed. It's all the more remarkable because apparent logic is being put to the service of making us have faith in things—things without necessarily the certainty of logic—which we didn't have faith in before. What matters is only that the new beliefs make us feel good. It seemingly doesn't matter that these new beliefs are *necessarily*, or in any abstract sense at all, *true*. Part of the optimism

---

[11]Ibid., p. 164.
[12]Ibid.

of the self-help guides is their shared conviction that we as worriers are susceptible to what looks like sense, ready to listen to what seem like arguments, and then ready sincerely to believe what we have been guided to think. Just because this all makes us, apparently, feel better.

It's true, as far as I see it, that an idea *can* suddenly appear in my head and change how I perceive things. This is one of the extraordinary events of the ordinary life of our minds. I'm thinking of moments when a new idea, apparently unbidden, floats into our heads and we realize that we *could* regard matters in a different way: "Oh! perhaps x *didn't* mean y when she spoke to me and it is me who has misunderstood what she meant"; "Oh! I dislike that trait in my grand-father but now I suddenly realize that this part of my behavior, which I have never connected with him, is really a version of what he does"; "Oh! I have just realized that I was assuming x was going to happen and actually doing things that would make it: I really could change the assumption and maybe x wouldn't occur." These are not illegitimate ideas. Yet where do they come from? From where do these "revelations" arise? It's one of the curious things about writing—sometimes even speaking—that sentences can end in ways we had never envisaged when we started them.[13] There's a mystery about that and a kind of wonder. There is something similarly unknown, and wonderful, about where human beings go in their own minds and how we can change unexpectedly from within when an unbidden idea occurs to us though we have no idea where it came from or how it got there.

Change can arise from inside our heads in a curious and almost mysterious way. But the views of others—their recommendations, suggestions, "cures"—are, in my experience, harder to admit. They easily feel coercive. Such views are more difficult to stay with, too;

---

[13]This idea is admirably discussed in Derek Attridge, *The Singularity of Literature* (London: Routledge, 2004).

more difficult to possess or inhabit for long. Where worriers are concerned, there's no guarantee that we'll take much notice of a new perspective for very long, especially when it comes from outside (and that includes from reading). The problem with the new perspective is that we may, in the end, simply not be able to believe it. I, in particular, find it hard to understand that belief can be manufactured, *argued for*, in the way the self-help books assume. Belief belongs in deeper places than reasoning and persuasion can easily reach.

I felt the truth of that recently, the trouble of arguing myself into a new belief, when I accidentally came across the idea of *acedia*. I thought for a few excited days: here's a new way of thinking about worry and mental troubles! I talked about it—I even became quite embarrassingly evangelical about it. My poor friends . . . The concept of *acedia*, or *accidie*, familiar to philosophers, theologians, and historians, comes not from the modern self-help books. It comes from the oldest of Christian monastic traditions. Correcting any tendency to think of the solitary or religious life in romanticized or sentimentalized terms, *acedia* is a reminder of a monk's troubles, his mental anguish, his recurrent problems, and his boredom. This is St Evagrius Ponticus (345–99), Christian monk and thinker, sometimes called Evagrius the Solitary, writing about *acedia* as a form of bad knowledge:

> The demon of *acedia*—also called the noonday demon—is the one that causes the most serious trouble of all. He presses his attack upon the monk about the fourth hour and besieges the soul until the eighth hour. First of all he makes it seem that the sun barely moves, if at all, and that the day is fifty hours long. Then he constrains the monk to look constantly out the windows, to walk outside the cell, to gaze carefully at the sun to determine how far it stands from the ninth hour [or lunchtime], to look this way and

now that to see if perhaps [one of the brethren appears from his cell]. Then too he instills in the heart of the monk a hatred for the place, a hatred for his very life itself, a hatred for manual labor. He leads him to reflect that charity has departed from among the brethren, that there is no one to give encouragement. Should there be someone at this period who happens to offend him in some way or other, this too the demon uses to contribute further to his hatred. This demon drives him along to desire other sites where he can more easily procure life's necessities, more readily find work and make a real success of himself. He goes on to suggest that, after all, it is not the place that is the basis of pleasing the Lord. God is to be adored everywhere. He joins to these reflections the memory of his dear ones and of his former way of life. He depicts life stretching out for a long period of time, and brings before the mind's eye the toil of the ascetic struggle and, as the saying has it, leaves no leaf unturned to induce the monk to forsake his cell and drop out of the fight. No other demon follows close upon the heels of this one (when he is defeated) but only a state of deep peace and inexpressible joy arise out of this struggle.[14]

St Evagrius isn't, clearly enough, describing worry. Nor is he describing depression (though perhaps there is some overlap with that). Yet he is thought-provoking because he offers a way, from the heart of the desert, of thinking about inner anxiety in general and how it not only can be, but ought to be, resisted.

Evagrius's point is to think of mental unease, of this particular kind, not as a trouble or sorrow, or as the bearer of some kind of gloomy truth. His point is to think of it as a species of temptation. *Acedia* is envisaged as that which distorts. It's a form of "bad

---

[14]Quoted in Kathleen Norris, *The Noonday Demon: A Modern Woman's Struggle with Soul-Weariness* (London: Lion, 2008), p. 13.

thought"; something that can be confused for truth but which is actually malign, an error. The central issue is that Evagrius recognizes weariness, frustration, or listlessness often involve thinking that there is a better life in doing something different from what we thought we cared about. He considers such a condition, primarily, is not our own fault (he personifies the trouble as coming from outside, as, in his terms, a "demon") but a test. These "demons" are distortions. They are *temptations* to devalue our lives, to mistrust what's around us, to believe erroneously that there are better ways of living than we live now. *Acedia* endeavors to turn to dust what we really, properly, care about. The experience is neither illness nor a glimpse of how things really are, nor some kind of problem with how we were brought up or the age we live in. It's a challenge. And, crucially, we can fight against it, like St George and the dragon. In Evagrius's understanding, the thoughts brought by *acedia* arrive unbidden from outside as things that test our confidence. Such thoughts challenge our security. They tempt us to believe in a mistake. And we can rid ourselves of them.

Can it be a *temptation* to believe that something is insecure or problematic or dangerous, when in fact it isn't? If nothing else, such an idea can put some distance between the worrier and the worry. Such an idea can create the chance of, so to speak, placing inverted commas around a worry so it becomes less our intimate companion. Is my worry about this or that a kind of inner *temptation* to believe something bad about myself that is disabling and disempowering? Can I usefully see worry as a kind of modern "demon" that isn't my fault but a *test* that I must pass? Can I usefully see a worry as a "bad thought," as "bad knowledge," a corrosive idea to which I can say no? The real answer to this, and the heart of my difficulty with the self-help books' well-meant advice, is that I once thought St Evagrius's idea was suggestive. On first acquaintance, I judged it helpful, refreshing, new. I thought, even, that this might be a key. I was ready to believe

Evagrius, to trust him, because he seemed wise. But I'm afraid I've drifted. I've stored his view in the back of my mind, where, I imagine, I'll gradually lose hold of it. I've crept furtively back to my habitual ways of thinking and believing. The worrier's mind is attached to how things used to be. The deep beliefs about the self, and worries of the future, aren't so frail, it seems to me, that they can be easily dislodged by what comes to us from without.

What's in Dr Leahy's book as well as in St Evagrius's writing is an invitation, at the profoundest level, not to think differently about our lives but to believe differently.

Yet there is a difference between truly believing something and believing in something that is true. St Evagrius's demons suggest that the grass is greener over there—but what if that *is*?

Worry might suggest to me that I'm not very good at my job and will be eventually found out, if I haven't been already. I could regard that as a negative temptation, a kind of self-destructive inner demon that I need to resist. I could act against that worry and construct on paper the terms of a healthier belief in better things. I could try to believe in something like Dr Leahy's recommendations for Darlene. But because a belief is more enabling doesn't make it more believable. Nor does it make it true. How can I be sure in the troubled sleepless hours that I was right? Such things aren't just a matter of argument or logic. Worry is simply one intrusive, insidious way in which we're exposed to the fact that, as human beings, and for all our faith in reason, for all our hopes to think of ourselves as logical creatures, we're really shaped by what we believe, including what we believe about ourselves. And, alas, the problem with those beliefs is that we believe them.

Worry lets us see not only our capacity to make ourselves the center of attention in our own minds. Worrying exposes what we really have faith in. Thinking about worry takes me into the unsettling territory of how believing plays a part in structuring my life even if I like to think of myself as a rational human being (and I'm not making any obvious comments here about religious faith). The more I think about what worries me, the more I come in front of questions about how I guide my behavior according, primarily, to beliefs that produce rational arguments and encourage particular behaviors but only after the fact. T. S. Eliot observed, about the art of criticism, that thought is over-challenged by inadequate knowledge:

> When there is so much to be known, when there are so many fields of knowledge in which the same words are used with different meanings, when everyone knows a little about a great many things, it becomes increasingly difficult for anyone to know whether he knows what he is talking about or not. And when we do not know, or when we do not know enough, we tend always to substitute emotions for thoughts.[15]

The golden age to which Eliot looks back, when it was possible to *know* everything and thus to be able to speak from knowledge, has long gone, even if it ever really existed. Yet it strikes me that there's a dim clue in Eliot's thinking about criticism that hints at a larger, rougher truth that has nothing to do with simply not knowing facts. It's about how we negotiate the world through our minds more generally. I substitute faith as well as emotion for what I do not know and, often enough, for *what I do not want to know* in the vast tangle of living.[16] In fact, reason regularly works—as I see it—to *justify* intuition, feelings, beliefs, which came first in the mind, regardless of whether we have "knowledge" or not. Reason supplies intuitions,

---

[15]"The Perfect Critic" (1920), most easily available in *Selected Prose of T.S. Eliot*, ed. Frank Kermode (London: Faber, 1975), pp. 50–8 (p. 55).

[16]There is a provocative study of the role of what we don't know in Stuart Firestein's *Ignorance: How It Drives Science* (Oxford: Oxford University Press, 2012).

convictions, faiths, and gut emotions with the cover of arguments and intellectual justifications. In the experience of worrying, reason is persistently secondary to a set of feelings and, however murkily, to a set of a priori convictions about ourselves and the world in which, and about which, we worry.

Worry springs from acts of belief. But perhaps I'm misleading about that "a priori." Beliefs have a backstory too. There are no doubt plenty of different explanations for how beliefs arrived and lodged themselves in my mind; plenty of explanations as to why I'm persuaded more by one belief than another. If reasoning comes after belief, there are presumably a good number of influences that establish themselves before belief. I don't mean to suggest, in other words, that we simply choose our beliefs about ourselves (and the world in which we live) as the modern self-help books seem to think. Culture, environment, upbringing, "natural inclinations," genetic inheritance, learned behaviors, and the nature of memory, are all forces contouring the susceptibility of an individual to this or that belief about themselves. Only the briefest acquaintance with the genetic revolutions of the twentieth century—everything those much-abused fruit flies tell us—suggests, not least, just how profoundly our minds are shaped by a kind of genetic memory communicated through our DNA. But the point, for me, remains that thinking about worry prompts questions not merely about "what" I believe. Such thinking obliges me to face the fact that my daily life is more guided by the nonreasoned, and my reasoning and behavior built on the nonreasoned, than I'm ordinarily willing to admit. That must be why many individuals approach worry not with reason but with charms.

The problem with the self-help books is, from this perspective, that they don't offer us any new spells. Worry belongs not primarily with the "think differently/believe differently" advice books. As a lived experience, worry's an intimate acquaintance of superstition. Worry secretly inhabits the domain of fetishes, the ascription of mysterious or religious attributes to objects or actions. It is accommodated with occult rites even in suburbia, on the freeway, in the department store. Thinking about worry is, in this respect, to discern some of the most apparently primitive and irrational habits of human minds in the heart of the modern world. The late nineteenth-century British anthropologist E. B. Tylor (1832–1917) formed the view, expressed in his *Primitive Culture: Researches into the Development of Mythology, Philosophy, Religion, Art, and Custom* (1871), that there were such things as "survivals" in advanced, civilized cultures. These were the remaining traditions, ways of thinking, or beliefs that belonged to the ancestral and primitive past but which had survived into the present. As a worrier, I can see something in this idea that he can hardly have meant.

Worry, at the beginning of the twentieth century, had a hint of the fashionable in its modernity. It was *de nous jours*. But modernity has long had a tendency to be attracted by magic.[17] It's as if, when we lurch into the future, realizing newness and what it brings, we need to keep more familiar, primal forms of human experience by our side. It's as if a new step forward summons up the most ancient memories of what human beings inherit from their ancestors. Such memories help us feel safe as we walk into the *terra incognita* of the new.

In the case of the machines, the buzz of the modern has been persistently accompanied in imaginative writing by languages that draw on ancient sources. Alexander Graham Bell (1847–1922) acquired the first patent for an electric telephone in 1876: remote communication across great distances was becoming possible. The

---

[17]An admirable literary study of this is Pamela Thurschwell, *Literature, Technology and Magical Thinking, 1880–1920* (Cambridge: Cambridge University Press, 2001).

telegraph had already allowed messages to be sent, using Samuel Morse's new code. But the telephone permitted voices to travel. The telephone, aptly from the Greek for "far voice," was, in the last decades of the nineteenth century, a new embodiment of the modern world, like the phonograph or sound recorder. But the telephone, like the phonograph, connected spookily with other "far voices," with ancient worlds seemingly long gone. In particular, the telephone became associated in the late nineteenth century with the speaking dead, the séance, and with its remote connections not across space but across the boundary between the living and the departed.

The great French Modernist Marcel Proust (1871–1922), in his multivolume novel *À la recherche du temps perdu* (1913–27), symptomatically imagines his narrator speaking to his grandmother on the phone. Their conversation is precious, a connection that matters. But "connection" has now become a word for a technical process as well as a human contact. And disconnection must follow soon in any conversation on the telephone. When the narrator's line is dead (how dark and terrifying our language for such technology is), he calls out his grandmother's name. But his voice sounds only in the empty air against the vacant silence of the line. A comparison with the ancient world springs, in turn, into the prose. "Grandma, Grandma," he calls, "like Orpheus, left alone, repeats the name of the dead [woman]."[18] The glitteringly modern merges with the mythological. Orpheus petitioned the powers of the underworld to allow his dead wife Eurydice, who had been killed by a snake, to return. The condition was that Orpheus must not look behind at his wife until they had both left the underworld. Disastrously, he turns and looks. She is lost for a

---

[18]"'Grand'mère, grand'mère,' comme Orphée, resté seul, repeté le nom de la morte," Marcel Proust, *Le côté de Guermantes* (Première partie), édition du texte, introduction, bibliographie par Elyane Dezon-Jones ([Paris]: Flammarion, 1987), p. 150. My translation.

second time, and forever. For Marcel Proust, one of the major figures of European literature, Eurydice's loss is like a telephone connection that's been broken.

Typewriters (and later computers) have seemed to have lives of their own; they are entangled with ancient conceptions of resident deities, attendant spirits. Ghosts came back and tapped at keys in late nineteenth-century fiction. Even now computers may seem to be "inhabited" by "gremlins," "trojans." The modern and the primitive, the contemporary and the residual stay together, as Stravinsky's quintessentially modern ballet *The Rite of Spring* (1913) drew on a vibrantly primitivist aesthetic. Some of the most highly experimental modern writers, including T. S. Eliot and the Anglo-Irish poet W. B. Yeats (1865–1939), were intrigued by the occult; by mystical ways of thinking, the cabbala, and ancient myth. Writing in the early part of the twentieth century, Yeats even came to believe that supernatural instructors were literally guiding him (though not very clearly). Through his wife's automatic writing, the Unknown Instructors, as he thought, offered him metaphors for poetry. The modern was full of spirits. T. S. Eliot's *The Waste Land* (1922) drew on mythological characters and scenes as part of a way of figuring the aridity of the contemporary world and the sources of its possible redemption. The British novelist and poet D. H. Lawrence (1885–1930) set about looking for more "primitive" and "authentic" ways of being and feeling against the superficialities of the early twentieth century. In multiple ways, a sense of the modern has revived the old and mysterious.

Oddly enough, worry itself, as the "disease of the age," as a particular feature of being modern, is hedged around with antique ways of thinking—or, rather, of believing. The worrier, often or not, is no stranger to invocations to powers that the contemporary rationalist might have thought ourselves rid. One of the most characteristic things that worriers do, though they would hardly say this themselves, is to act as if they are trying to win the favor of invisible and punitive forces. We seem to be trying, without saying as much, to placate great and dangerous Gods that have no names, no forms of communication, and very little mercy.

Worry breeds ritual. It's contained—so we hope—by ceremony. A friend of mine can rarely leave the house without a brief routine of checking; this routine exceeds the boundaries of the commonsensical. Helen will, for instance, check that the electric kettle is off. Sensible enough? Yes, but she will check it even though she pulls out the plug whenever she has finished using it. Helen needs to check not only that the plug really is out of the wall but that the kettle is facing the right direction. If it isn't, then that is—to her—a sign that something is or will be awry. Does she think, in some sealed lumber room of her mind, that the errant kettle might somehow magically start to boil if it is not turned the right way? And is "think" quite the right word here for this seemingly deep-rooted belief in forces that are external to regular physical law, implacable, ruthless?

Likewise, Helen must go upstairs and pick up her hair straighteners in the spare bedroom before she leaves the house. This may be ostensibly to check that the straighteners are not still hot (you can't tell just by looking at them and they make no sound). Helen will do this even when she knows that those straighteners (which she infrequently uses anyway) aren't plugged in and have not been used for days. They're stone cold. She must pick them up and put them down again before she can relax, or, at least, feel sufficiently secure to leave the house. At least, I *think* that is what is passing through her mind. It would be quite impossible for me to ask. She would be horribly offended. She would almost certainly say nothing other than "I just wanted to check." The deeper matters of what occurs in her consciousness I can only guess at. I'm certainly only guessing when I suggest that it's inconceivable that Helen would fail to go through this leaving-the-house ritual. I'm also only guessing when I say that it seems some obligations to the higher powers must never be unfulfilled.

My friend isn't weird. She has a happy family, a successful job, a good degree from a good university. She's an ordinary worrier and a charming, charismatic person. She's hardly the only individual to try to control the future, in some modest but significant way, through ritual. Her private superstitions aren't hers alone. The worrier, sensible and sane in many ways, lives part of his or her life superstitiously as well as surreptitiously. We worriers, whether we like it or not, are subconscious believers, often believers who try to deny that we are believers, in forces that have their own requirements, and which will, we guess, punish defaulters drastically. We worriers might be suffering from a modern condition. But our tools for dealing with it seem to be the same as those of those who built the barrows and the stone circles.

What *are* these powers? What or who does the worrier really think he or she is placating through these little rituals? (Again, "think" isn't quite the right word here.) Such rituals are, certainly, indicative of how deeply the need for rites remains. They are, perhaps, indicative of something of the lack of control worriers feel they have over their lives since they must keep on their side unknown forces that have the capacity, apparently, to chastise the most minimal of transgressions. There is something of a cold-blooded, inflexible tyranny here, of powers with neither pity nor court of appeal. Ariel in Shakespeare's late play, *The Tempest*, makes the mistake of speaking about being freed when silence and submission are required. Prospero, Ariel's master, remarks: "If thou more murmur'st, I will rend an oak, | And peg thee in his knotty entrails till | Thou hast howled away twelve winters."[19] That's the sort of violent, vengeful authority, spurred by the

---

[19] *The Tempest*, 1:2:295–7.

most minor of infractions, we worriers have in mind. These powers may be functions of our readiness to feel guilty about our lives or displaced forms of recognition, at some level, of the precarious nature of our existence in a threatening environment. These powers may be the by-products of deep insecurities and the strange children of a hope that, somehow, we can survive if we do the right thing, if we sacrifice to the right God. They may be, too, the most curious mental "survivals" from ancestors whose names we can never know but whose bodies, genetically, we still inhabit. These powers are indicative of the unknown nature of the world that the worrier recognizes and the lack of real control we have over a future in which uncertainty is assured.

Some of the most remarkable histories of human distress have concerned serious mental illness. But these stories, well narrated, have been compelling—uncomfortably, perhaps, but compelling all the same. My colleague, Stuart Murray, wrote a brave, humane, and luminous book about autism that he called *Representing Autism: Culture, Narrative, Fascination* (2008). And that word "fascination" has fascinated me. It's brave because it admits allure. The direst forms of mental illness have allure too, there's no denying it. Lewis Wolpert's *Malignant Sadness: The Anatomy of Depression*, one of the most admired British books from the inside of depression, includes some of Wolpert's own moving personal history of "depression" (the inverted commas are meant to suggest his concern about depression's lack of clear definition) as well as a good deal of scientific exploration about what the condition really is. It makes for a gripping psychological exploration. William Styron's *Darkness Visible: A Memoir of Madness* (1990) is a fuller narration, and equally absorbing, written with a novelist's expertise that carries the reader into the Stygian gloom of what depression might be like. The US psychologist Kay Redfield Jamison's *An Unquiet Mind: A Memoir of Moods and Madness* (1995), a remarkable autobiography of life with "bipolar disorder," is a kind of mental-health thriller, full of highs and lows, tension and recovery. Jamison recounts the drama of living daily with a condition that periodically drives a sufferer into something like a new version of Thomas De Quincey's *Confessions of an English Opium Eater* (1821), with its starkly divided acknowledgment of joys and horrors. The tempests of serious mental illness, as Shakespeare's *King Lear* made clear at the beginning of the seventeenth century, are the raw material of potentially captivating histories, episodes with inbuilt fascination. Here, with all its discomforting ethical problems, is spectacle.

Worry makes no best-selling autobiographies. It can turn conversation into tedium with effortless ease. Yet for all its inability to suggest *King Lear*, worry has its dramas too. For all worry's usually mundane dullness and repetitive ordinariness, for all its weary familiarity as a countermelody to daily life, worry flirts with romance, tragedy, and the mythic. It belongs with episodes of epic, with scenes of terrible confrontations between human beings and the Gods. The world worry calls up is, actually, extraordinarily strange. The worrier's tale is a revenge tragedy waiting to happen. It's a story of the continual temptations of a malign fate to disempower and crush. It's a narrative of the private superstitions of reasonable people who endeavor to ward off wildly unreasonable, punitive retribution from powers that delight— the worrier supposes—in punishing the smallest of their errors. The worrier's tale takes place in an environment of staggering mercilessness. All this goes on quietly in the background of daily life, almost invisible to anyone else, behind the espresso cups and next to the cutlery.

Worry reveals. It enables me to see some of the ways in which "normal" life is populated with the bizarre and how easy it is to confuse "ordinary" life with some bland conception of reasonable level-headedness, of logical behavior, of a commonplace range of commonplace emotions, of sensible plans and sensible decisions. To look into the heart of mundane worry is to see a little more clearly than usual something of the real weirdness of what many people do in their heads every day.

Far away from the ordinary world of worry, there are objections to the labels of modern psychiatry. The Scottish psychiatrist R. D. Laing (1927–89) challenged what were then orthodox assumptions about mental illness, particularly psychosis. He argued that the worldviews of the "psychotic" should be treated with dignity because they were legitimate ways of experiencing life not simply symptoms of mental conditions that were outside normality, beyond acceptance, far from regular ways of being. That controversial erasure of a clear borderline between "normal" life and that previously categorized as insane continues among other writers on mental health. It's still provocative. Richard Bentall, for instance, questions the diagnostic terms of psychotic illness and schizophrenia in an effort to free understanding of mental illness from what he sees as remaining false categories. Such categories have often been inherited, he points out, from the psychiatry of Europe in the nineteenth century and never comprehensively revised. Part of Bentall's argument in *Madness Explained: Psychosis and Human Nature* (2003) concerns the ways in which "ordinariness" and "madness" are hard to separate. He's intrigued by day-to-day "symptoms" of mental illness that fall into diagnostic categories, and which appear in the DSM, and yet do not prompt a diagnosis and are usually integrated into our expectations of what normal life is like.

Do regular people experience psychotic symptoms ordinarily? A comprehensive survey by Allen Tien of hallucination, one of the formal symptoms of psychosis, reported in 1991 that somewhere between 11 and 13 percent of 18,000 participants in a population survey had experienced hallucinations at some time in their lives. Thirteen percent! Delusional beliefs, another official symptom of the psychotic, were known far beyond the number of people formally diagnosed with a serious mental health disorder: "Estimates of the number of people in the USA who had had 'abduction experiences' [believing that they have been kidnapped by aliens before being returned to earth] have been as high as 3.7 million."[20] Of course, "delusional" depends on your point of view. The fundamental tenets of the major world religions will look delusional to the skeptic or atheist while seeming the brightest of reality to the believer. For hypomania (mood swings), a similar if less provocative picture has been documented. In the Zurich canton of Switzerland, the psychiatrist Jules Angst reported that 4 percent of the population had experienced "mild episodes of mania." After another survey 14 years later, the figure for those who had experienced the official diagnostic criteria for hypomania had risen to five and a half percent. Some 11.3 percent had also experienced lesser or "subdiagonistic" hypomanic symptoms. That's a very large number indeed.[21]

However much they require more analysis and research, such figures hint at the trouble there is in drawing an absolute line between the "insane" and the "sane" in clinical terms. Fiction has told us that already. Mary Elizabeth Braddon's sensation novel *Lady Audley's Secret* (1862) had already made readers wonder about whether madness was a category error, a convenient label for disposing of those who resisted the normal requirements of polite behavior or were otherwise inconvenient. And contemporary fiction continues to probe the difference between the mentally ill and the sane. The British writer Adam Foulds's novel about the mental health of the English poets John Clare and Alfred Tennyson, *The Quickening Maze* (2009), leaves the reader with no decisive sense of where the line might be. Jonathan Franzen's novel of a calamitously dysfunctional family, *The Corrections* (2002), allows a reader to reflect on the destructive behavior of the apparently "normal" in relation to those with clinical

---

[20]Bentall, *Madness Explained*, p. 100.

[21]Figures and details from Bentall, *Madness Explained*, p. 103.

diagnoses, particularly a father with Parkinson's. The debate in this novel about Gary's "depression," intriguingly told from Gary's perspective, does little to clear up where the divisions between the normal and the pathological are. Admitting such confusions seems to me at once freeing and terrifying. On that division, the treatment of many men and women both now and in the past has depended. Cruelty and violence have policed the border, good intentions and bad. Lives have been saved or destroyed, human beings released and confined, on either side of it—and on what evidence?

If we can't be wholly certain who's mad, we can hardly be assured of who's sane. If millions of people experience hallucinations but aren't labeled psychotic, it seems less surprising to say that worriers, getting on with their ordinary days, have some innate, peculiar, and undisclosed belief in the Eumenides. The bounds of the "normal" are wide. The worrier's mind is—I glamorize it—like great Gothic architecture. It's full of invention, fantasy, and asymmetry, replete with the consoling and the shocking, crisscrossed with the grotesquely comic. It has something of the real and something of the magical, the supernatural and the crazily fantastic about it. The worrier's mind involves monumental faith and it can never be seen all at once. It is strange and wonderful, shocking and peculiar. If sanity, in any way, is an ability to function adequately in the day-to-day world, then worry tells us that so-called sanity embraces the strange in a way that makes the strange normal. A crude notion of "ordinariness" or a rough conception of what it is to be "sane" flattens for me the real peculiarity of life on the other side of silence. I don't have any very adequate understanding of what "sanity" is. But I do know that it seems we must live with a great myth of the logical, ordinary, and controlled nature of normality, even as, in our deepest being, we worriers know that to be misleading.

The British psychologist and writer Adam Phillips, in *Going Sane* (2005), tries to make good the absence of discussion about sanity in the face of exhaustive efforts to get to the bottom of madness. Part of his claim is that sanity exists in having the right belief about oneself. From depression, Phillips says:

> We get a sense of the sane self as loving itself in the right way, of having what is considered to be appropriate self-regard: the kind of feeling about oneself that sustains one's appetite for life. This vitality, moreover, is likely to issue in finding objects of love, and then having the wherewithal to protect one's cake and eat it. [. . .] Sanity means loving oneself in exactly the right way, or knowing exactly what it is about oneself that is worth loving. This means, essentially, having a self-belief in a picture, or a story, or a set of preferred fantasies—to love.[22]

Rather unexpectedly, reading Phillips, I'm back to where I started with my difficulties with the self-help books. Here I am again, in the midst of a discussion of the sane, returning to the idea of having the "right belief" about myself, and back with the fundamental question of the difference between believing in something because it's helpful and believing in it because it's true. I'm back to the territories of faith, and the rewriting of creeds, without real or compelling guidance about how to make those new beliefs happen or, more importantly, how to make them believable because truthful. Phillips, I notice, is daringly candid in accepting a "set of preferred fantasies" he thinks we need to believe in. He can obviously deal, in a way I can't, with the fact that we should believe in something enabling *even if we know it is made up*.

I'm back, in other words, with the great mystery of how to believe in a belief that isn't mine.

---

[22]Adam Phillips, *Going Sane* (London: Hamish Hamilton, 2005), p. 184.

3

The time is out of joint

Hamlet, 1:5:189

Reason might follow after belief in the "act" of worrying and in this respect worry may be like many forms rational activity—anterior, belated, trying to catch up with feelings, beliefs, and intuitions that took place earlier. It might also be true that belief and reasoning in the experience of worry have a longer and more awkward history of conflict. It might be that the bonding of worry with belief is, apart from anything else, a paradoxical after-effect of religious belief's displacement. The Danish philosopher Søren Kierkegaard (1813–55) thought that the religious life—the highest he could conceive—was one of continual mental anxiety. The religious man was persistently caught between his own desires and the dictates of the absolute in which he believed. Part of the deepest cause of anxiety was produced by that division, a version of the tension between desire for the self and recognition of a higher good.

It might be truer to say that one of the deep causes of worry isn't the trouble caused by a conflict between an individual's desire and his or her sense of a higher good but by the very fact we, as individuals, can reason about our desires at all. When I consider our modern belief that we have politically and morally some form of *right* to have our individual desires fulfilled, or at least taken into account, I can see that there's more likelihood of trouble. Choosing for ourselves is part of what the contemporary world tells us is a fundamental principle of contemporary society, a feature of its success. But it's not success alone. This is a chapter about the ways in which we've inherited a world that privileges reason, despite what I've said in the previous chapter, as a defining feature of being human. To that, problematically, we've added a whole raft of assumptions about thinking and choosing "freely" within which worry has been able to flourish more than ever.

As a practice of the mind, worry is only possible in a world of choice. It's even more possible when human beings think, in turn, that they have the capacity, let alone the right, to choose for themselves. Worry is the inevitable handmaiden of our conviction that we should make our own decisions. "Depression," says Andrew Solomon in his generous book, *The Noonday Demon: An Anatomy of Depression* (2001), "is the flaw in love."[1] Worry, on the other hand, is a flaw in reason. It's reason's downside; it's the collateral damage reason does. The birth of worry, abstractedly speaking, could be said to happen at the moment of a culture's shift from unquestioning faith in omnipotent powers to *thought* or *reasoning* as the way of understanding human existence within the world. Despite everything I've said previously about worry and faith, it's true that worry is the offspring, unintended and unwelcome, of a shift from believing in supernatural beings that absolutely control to believing in the strength of the human mind and its own capacity to think things through. Worry is the unhappy child of a turn from the Gods to man. It is, at one level, the result of the broadest shift in human culture from heart to mind; from a faith in an abstract fate to the world of human selection; from the Age of Faith to the Age of Enlightenment; from the ideal to the real; from the skies to the earth.

---

[1] Andrew Solomon, *The Noonday Demon: An Anatomy of Depression* (London: Vintage, 2002), p. 10.

Worry becomes possible only when a human being believes that events don't have a predetermined outcome, already chosen in the mind of some inscrutable divinity. Worry becomes possible when Olympus is merely a mountain. It becomes possible only in a world where we must fend for ourselves. Worry flourishes where human beings believe they can decide outcomes for themselves from a reasoned assessment of what the options might be; an assessment, perhaps, which tries to take everything into account. Worry flourishes even more when we think that there is a *right* decision to be made about the future and we have to use our own powers to discern it rather than rely on divine authority. And when the reasoned assessment that tries to take everything into account endeavors to accommodate how we as human beings *feel*, to address the question of what makes us *emotionally* secure, calm, and happy, then worry has an even surer foothold. Such "everything-into-account" calculations require, almost always, that "reason" must recognize not only arguments but also the unreasonable, or the beyond reason, too. We have given our minds a lot of work to do. And all this—all the attempts to balance interests in choosing the best way forward—is the perfect breeding ground for sleepless nights. If worry has a "short" or "local" history that concerns its emergence into language at the beginning of the twentieth century, it has a long history too.

The most powerful features of the history of the human mind, of the intellectual changes that have made us who we are, can only be mapped in emblematic history, in mythological accounts of our genesis. It's tempting to plot the moment of worry's birth and to pin it down in time: it happened *there*, it happened *then*. I would certainly like to know *exactly* where and when Pandora opened her annoying box of troubles. I'd also like to know, by the way, if what was left at the bottom of that wretched box was "hope" or, more worryingly, "anticipation." Anticipation, of course, can be with pleasure or with fear.

The idea of a beginning, or a turning point, is attractive to the way we narrate history. The appeal of beginnings, of being able to say "this attitude began *here*," or this "new way of looking at the world had its origin in *this*," was well recognized by the British novelist George Eliot (1819–80), a writer fascinated by the interplay of forces that permit and constrain human choice. "Men can do nothing without the make-believe of a beginning,"[2] she sagely said. And men can do nothing, either, without the narrative of how that beginning *relates* to the present. The temptation to find starting points is the temptation to create foundation myths, to fashion emblems that offer essences not empirical truths. The temptation to see those points as origins requires an assumption that history works always in some kind of ordered, sequential, developmental, or evolutionary way. The make-believe of a beginning involves not only a myth of a starting point but the myth that history is story-shaped: that history accommodates nothing significant that is random, uneven, broken, accidental, or unaccounted for. Worry and its history is not an exception to this. And the mythological imaginings of the "birth of thinking" are more or less inexhaustible.

The ancient Greeks, with their highly sophisticated philosophical reasoning, have a ready claim to be considered architects of the modern "thinking mind" even though they were forgotten for the long centuries of the Dark Ages. The fathers of Western philosophy, the Greeks can be easily imagined as the champions of thought against ignorance, the blind groping of mere belief in a world ruled by all-powerful divinities. Is that where thinking began? The British Prime Minister and Homeric scholar W. E. Gladstone (1809–98) was not alone in declaring in Homer's works "lie the beginnings of the intellectual life of the world."[3] The end of the medieval period in

---

[2] George Eliot, *Daniel Deronda*, 4 vols (Edinburgh: Blackwood, 1876), i.3.
[3] W. E. Gladstone, *Studies on Homer and the Homeric Age*, 3 vols (Oxford: Oxford University Press, 1858), i.14.

Europe and the beginning of the Renaissance has served as another closer and popular moment of the "(re-)birth of thought," with a few glimmers of usually persecuted reason before it. "Renaissance Humanism" and the recovery of Aristotle make the argument clearer, as do the secular interests of the Renaissance artists, with their use of perspective to emphasize a human view of the world rather than God's. The philosophers and encyclopedists of eighteenth-century France and the whole experience of the Aufklärung, the European Enlightenment, constitute other ready emblems of the so-called birth of the modern world, the establishment of the thinking mind against "unreasoned" faith in invisible forces that neither required nor rewarded thought. The work of the Enlightenment might be seen completed, in turn, by the solidification of the "scientific method" in the nineteenth century and the apparent abandonment of faith-over-thinking for the new secular sciences emblematized by the publication of Charles Darwin's *The Origin of Species* in 1859 and the panoply of empirical investigation that defined the intellectual life of the scientific age.

There are good reasons for objecting to every one of these. There are better reasons for objecting to this whole business of identifying moments of such apparently universal change of mind in the first place. History, of course, doesn't work like this. And then, as if this wasn't enough, there are different moral evaluations of what I'm describing. The Islamic tradition, for a start, would hardly recognize what I am talking about, seeing in this account of the "birth of thought" a history not of triumphant enlightenment but the emergence of decadence and a turn from God. Yet these emblematic moments of change have a powerful meaning. They've significance even if they're not "authentic" or empirically true. Like pictures of ourselves we know to be false, we apparently can't do without them. They are, as George Eliot would no doubt have said, among the make-believes with which we can't dispense because their symbolic meaning can't be lost. Some things really are too important to get right. The implications of these myths are well-embedded in our sense of who we are as human beings and modern human beings in particular. Mere factuality mustn't be allowed to stand in their way. The exchange of a world of unthinking belief for a world of independent thought is an important explanatory myth of modern human history even if we can't plot it, or say it is, in any simple sense, correct. That alteration from faith to reason is the great Western story of our coming-to-ourselves; the capacious myth of the birth of the individual; the consoling story of our own importance and the legitimacy and integrity of our "right" to think for ourselves.

The French philosopher René Descartes (1596–1650) divided up those who really existed from those who did not on the basis of a capacity to think. He did this with one of the most famous (and, it seems to me, most arrogant) philosophical statements in modern history—"je pense, donc je suis": "I think, therefore I am." Descartes has often been understood as trying to divide human beings from animals as well as declaring his skeptical hand to "unthinking" religious believers. But he was also, emblematically, describing the terms from which worry would grow into and from the secular, reasoning mind. The acceptance of the primacy of thought in evaluating options is the eye of the needle through which the thin, ashen figure of worry slipped among us because the necessity to think for ourselves allows, of course, the chance of getting it wrong. Apparently repudiating faith in favor of the reasoning processes of the mind, Descartes's phrase clinched—or re-clinched—the condition in which worry could exist. He might have written something else instead. He might have written: "I worry, therefore I am." But I don't think that would have proved very different in the end.

This imaginary but necessary conception of the enabling turn from "blind" faith to reason, to the idea that we have *choices* that we can *think* about, that we can do our own thing according to our own lights, can influence even how we talk about our own histories. The privileging of independent thought, of the freely thinking mind, is so powerful a cultural narrative that it can easily become, literally, autobiographical. The first moment that I actually thought about something independently and freely, if I recall it now, is a clear episode in my head. I've persuaded myself, certainly, that I remember it accurately. I was 17. How had I managed to get those O-levels without ever once using my mind properly? Never mind. I could say to myself now that I'd never really done any thinking at all but was working in the boxes I had been given, believing what I had been told. I was crossing a road in Wolverhampton, near an untidy street with a few struggling and seedy shops, and I was fretting about one of our A-level texts. It was Shakespeare's *King Lear*, of all things. That's not a play about reasoned action, ironically enough. I was "thinking" of what our teacher would want us to say about a particular question when suddenly it occurred to me that the question itself was misleading. I thought for a few moments about how it could be looked at from a different perspective, gathering some lines in the play in my head that didn't fit the assumption behind what we had been asked. Then I suddenly realized what I was doing. I had reached, without warning signs or preparation, the edge of a cliff. I was high above a murky pool I couldn't see. I was on the verge of questioning something I had been told: and what a dreadful mess I could get into if that continued! I had a dim but dreadful apprehension of the personal, intellectual, and no doubt moral chaos that would result in my realization that I could think about things for myself. Perhaps thinking for myself was exactly what my teachers had been hoping for all along. But just at that moment such independence felt like a terrifying act of rebellion; an attempt to put myself in harm's way. I had to stop it and it took a couple of years before I started it again.

I *think* this story's true. Until I considered it for this book, I'd never questioned its authenticity. But now I wonder if I'm illustrating merely that I have been persuaded by our great cultural narrative of what's important about being a human being. Am I simply living evidence of how difficult it is to get away from that Birth-of-Reason narrative as the exciting, new, and precious event in growing up not only as a species but as an individual? Am I celebrating the idea of the beginning of independent reason because I have internalized personally the cultural tales I have just been mulling over? Perhaps I'm only a willing collaborator in an *ur*-story that feels natural and right but which in truth has been written for me by the age in which I live. My story mimics on the smallest scale the most important narrative of the intellectual life: the emergence of independent-minded, "free" human beings, whose worth and dignity lies, when they finally realize it, in their capacity to decide things "for themselves." But what's most obvious to me, retelling what I think it my own history, is just how troubling that realization was.

It's easy to fantasize an ancient society free not only from worry but from the *possibility* of worry. This would be a culture with a firm conviction in destiny that can't admit of trepidation because the results of all things are beyond mortal control. For the ancient Greeks, the hands that controlled men's lives were literal. Clotho spun the thread of life for each individual while her sister, Lachesis, measured its length: Atropos, the third, had human beings' futures in her hands because she decided when to cut the thread. With its severing, a man or woman's life ended. As far as worry is concerned, I suppose we worriers should regard those as the good old days. If they weren't free from worry they were at least free from any purpose to worrying. Why should we fret when the Gods have everything in hand? Why be anxious when there's nothing you can do to change the outcome the deities have decided or will decide? Having no power to choose, we had better enjoy our life until the Gods cut the thread.

Yet it's impossible to find evidence, I think, of a real, literal time and place when this might have been true. As I think about the remains of the ancient literature, and over the visual testimony of more recent times, I can't help but be struck by the repetition of the same bald fact. That once a human being is able to think—to process and consider, to adjudicate and ponder in their own heads, even in the context of deep religious faith—there's difficulty. The possibilities of worry are created by the very capacity to ruminate, to assess, to weigh up, to wonder. In a sad way, it seems, being a modern worrier is just, in the most general of terms and across all the testimonies of our history, the moth-eaten sign of being human. *Je m'inquiète donc je suis*: I worry, therefore I am.

The great epics of the ancient Mediterranean, for a start, offer different accounts of why a faith in the Gods, a belief in the power of destiny, of fate itself, left men and women insecure and loaded with troubles. Their authors could not *imagine* a world ruled by the Gods without fretting because having the power to think, to reflect, to meditate, meant the capacity to be bothered. In the ancient Greek epic of the *Iliad*, Homer's poem about the Trojan War probably written around the eighth-century BC, there's a celebrated example of what might seem on first thought to be the mind-of-faith, a man who ought not to speculate even when a God-appointed death is approaching. This large section of the *Iliad*, Book VI, is from Samuel Butler's late nineteenth-century translation. Hector, the noble Trojan warrior, is about to leave his home and his wife Andromache, to fight in the Trojan War:

Hector smiled as he looked upon the boy, but he did not speak, and Andromache stood by him weeping and taking his hand in her own. "Dear husband," said she, "your valour will bring you to destruction; think on your infant son, and on my hapless self who ere long shall be your widow—for the Achaeans will set upon you in a body and kill you. It would be better for me, should I lose you, to lie dead and buried, for I shall have nothing left to comfort me when you are gone, save only sorrow. I have neither father nor mother now. Achilles slew my father when he sacked Thebe, the goodly city of the Cilicians. He slew him, but did not for very shame despoil him; when he had burned him in his wondrous armour, he raised a barrow over his ashes and the mountain nymphs, daughters of aegis-bearing Jove, planted a grove of elms about his tomb. I had seven brothers in my father's house, but on the same day they all went within the house of Hades. Achilles killed them as they were with their sheep and cattle. My mother—her who had been queen of all the land under Mt. Placus—he brought hither with the spoil, and freed her for a great sum, but the archer-queen Diana took her in the house of your father. Nay—Hector—you who to me are father, mother, brother, and dear husband—have mercy upon me; stay here upon this wall; make not your child fatherless, and your wife a widow; as for the host, place them near the fig-tree, where the city can be best scaled, and the wall is weakest. Thrice have the bravest of them come thither and assailed it, under the two Ajaxes, Idomeneus, the sons of Atreus, and the brave son of Tydeus, either of their own bidding, or because some soothsayer had told them."

And Hector answered, "Wife, I too have thought upon all this, but with what face should I look upon the Trojans, men or women, if I shirked battle like a coward? I cannot do so: I know nothing save to fight bravely in the forefront of the Trojan host and win renown alike for my father and myself. Well do I know that the day will surely come when mighty Ilius shall be destroyed with

Priam and Priam's people, but I grieve for none of these—not even for Hecuba, nor King Priam, nor for my brothers many and brave who may fall in the dust before their foes—for none of these do I grieve as for yourself when the day shall come on which some one of the Achaeans shall rob you for ever of your freedom, and bear you weeping away. It may be that you will have to ply the loom in Argos at the bidding of a mistress, or to fetch water from the springs Messeis or Hypereia, treated brutally by some cruel task-master; then will one say who sees you weeping, 'she was wife to Hector, the bravest warrior among the Trojans during the war before Ilius.' On this your tears will break forth anew for him who would have put away the day of captivity from you. May I lie dead under the barrow that is heaped over my body ere I hear your cry as they carry you into bondage."

He stretched his arms towards his child, but the boy cried and nestled in his nurse's bosom, scared at the sight of his father's armour, and at the horse-hair plume that nodded fiercely from his helmet. His father and mother laughed to see him, but Hector took the helmet from his head and laid it all gleaming upon the ground. Then he took his darling child, kissed him, and dandled him in his arms, praying over him the while to Jove and to all the gods. "Jove," he cried, "grant that this my child may be even as myself, chief among the Trojans; let him be not less excellent in strength, and let him rule Ilius with his might. Then may one say of him as he comes from battle, 'The son is far better than the father.' May he bring back the blood-stained spoils of him whom he has laid low, and let his mother's heart be glad."

With this he laid the child again in the arms of his wife, who took him to her own soft bosom, smiling through her tears. As her husband watched her his heart yearned towards her and he caressed her fondly, saying, "My own wife, do not take these things too bitterly to heart. No one can hurry me down to Hades before my time, but if a man's hour is come, be he brave or be he coward, there is no escape for him when he has once been born. Go, then, within the house, and busy yourself with your daily duties, your loom, your distaff, and the ordering of your servants; for war is man's matter, and mine above all others of them that have been born in Ilius."[4]

Hector speaks about the difficult certainty of a world ruled by the Gods: "there is no escape for [a man] when he has once been born," he says. Hector's final point to his wife is that the Gods choose and that there's no point in trying to resist their will. We are, all of us, bound to decisions made by others beyond the earth and our own judgments and anxieties are as nothing in comparison with the steely hand of fate, the decrees of the powers above us. What is right (or certainly what is going to happen) has already been decided and, perhaps, if there is a bad decision it's because of the corruption of, or the infighting among, the Gods. It's nothing to do with human choice or human hope or what humans have tried to do for themselves. What's the use of worrying?

But Homer *doesn't* exactly say that. He cannot really envisage Hector thinking his acceptance of the Gods is, emotionally, enough. At one level, this is merely to say that there could be little affecting interest in a poem that told of simple acceptance. Literature needs tension and it needs suffering. But there's a deeper point about *how hard* it is even to envisage a world where, if there's no "rational" cause for worry, there is no rumination on sorrows, no thinking about implications, no wondering exactly what the future will bring. The

---

[4]This is most easily accessible on http://sacred-texts.com/cla/homer/ili/index.htm (last accessed January 23, 2014).

hero's noble courage in epic destiny has not stopped Andromache fretting about Hector's death and neither has it stopped Hector. Before he explicitly announces that he has no choice, Hector has tried to reason with Andromache, as if argument and explanation and consolation do have a place amid a world where, supposedly, the Gods have already assumed the power to decide. Hector admits that Andromache's anxieties have been his own: "Wife, I too have thought upon all this." If in the end Hector doesn't question the Gods as rulers of destiny, he finds that no relief to sorrow. Because he can think, he can suffer. Homer, the thinking man, can't envisage that Hector's turn to the Gods means there's no reason to do anything than blankly meet one's destiny. Jean Restout's painting *Hector Taking Leave of Andromache* (1728)[5] magnified that anxiety even amid Hector's noble faith in the Gods many centuries later. The Trojan hero looks uncertainly up to the skies.

In the literature of the ancient Greeks' inheritors, there's a similar issue. The question of imagining the Gods' roles in human life— whether it is worth worrying about the future or not—is a major matter of Virgil's *Aeneid*, written around 29–19 BC. A poem about the founding of Rome after the fall of Troy, the *Aeneid* is a searching account of the nature of imperialism, of the burdens of leadership, and the sorrows that attend on even the best-lived lives. It's a peculiarly melancholy work. But it's also about the "mechanism" of the Gods, the role of the supernatural in human life, and a robust challenge to any simplistic notion of fate that makes men and women merely counters within the plans of the deities. It's true that Virgil perceives the Gods as intimately involved in human lives—Vulcan constructs weapons for Aeneas, for instance, and Venus delivers them to him in Book VIII.

---

[5] *Les Adieux de Hector et d'Andromaque* is currently in the collection of Mrs Ruth Blumka, New York.

But the Gods themselves are divided. This is no world where what will happen next is straightforward, let alone certain, and so, for the thinking man, there are grounds for concern. Juno, for one, supports Aeneas's enemies. In Book IX, before the battle, both Aeneas and his opponent Turnus defy each other with their supernatural support. Turnus is cowed neither by the Gods' support nor the portents that attend his enemy. "I too have oracles | Backing me," Turnus says.[6] The reader can't fail to notice that faith in supernatural beings proposes no certainty in Virgil's world of opposition, counterclaim, and error. No wonder, in Cecil Day-Lewis's luminous translation, Aeneas at the beginning of Book VIII is "much agitated by surging worries,| His mind in feverish conflict, tosses from one side to the other, | Twisting and turning all ways to find a way past his dilemma."[7] Virgil's words, mediated by a twentieth-century poet, speak effortlessly to the modern worrier with a sharp realization of kinship across two thousand years.

A faith in fate, sincerely and wholly believed, exposes choice as illusory. Yet it's hard to believe that real breathing human beings ever lived in such a world. Troubles are with us as soon as we express our thoughts at all, including our thoughts about faith structures in which, supposedly, we might not need to think that much. We have to fantasize far remoter history than that of ancient Greek and Rome (and they are hardly remote anyway) and to fantasize without any evidence whatsoever if we're going to come up with a society that'd given itself up so completely to the rule of powers in the sky that human beings didn't care. Were the cave painters like that? Perhaps the earliest manifestations of *homo sapiens*? Perhaps, perhaps—but who can tell?

---

[6]Virgil, *The Aeneid*, p. 253. IX.136–7.
[7]Ibid., pp. 220–1. VIII.19–21.

In turn, there's a more modern iconography of worry. It's tempting to think of many representations of human thought in the visual arts as haunted by the shadows of bother. Visual presentations of thinking don't obviously discriminate between thought and trepidation, thinking and worry. Auguste Rodin's famous status of *The Thinker* (1902) might be an anxious philosopher for the modern world despite the heroic certainty of his muscular form. Looking at Rodin's masterpiece, we can worry about what it is, exactly, the thinker is considering and is puzzled by. We can worry about what the thinker is worried about, because we don't know. But we can also recognize Rodin's acceptance, simply enough, that thinking's hard. Earlier, the Italian Renaissance's imagining of the act of using our minds offered other suggestive examples of a conviction that the business of reasoning was fraught. Thinking may be the privilege of human beings but it isn't happiness. From fifteenth- and sixteenth-century Italy are some of the best presentations, from the heart of the Renaissance, of the awareness that fretfulness is the companion of mind, that trouble is part of our nature as a ruminating species.

Piero della Francesca's small painting from 1451 of *S. Girolamo e uno devoto* (*St Jerome with a Follower*) now hangs in an awkward space in the Accademia Gallery in Venice. Piero's greens have oxidized into a murky brown. But it's the concentrating face of the saint that intrigues me. This small picture is ambivalent about authority and thought, about obedience and freedom to question. Is St Jerome, an intellectual of the Church, who is often depicted at work in his study, speaking or listening in Piero della Francesca's work? Is he teaching or reflecting on what the disciple has asked? Is he looking for help in the Bible on his knee or for authority on which to base his judgment? Is he trying to decide for himself based on what he knows and thinks? Whether this is a scene of instruction or discussion, of debate or the mere assertion of what's legitimate to think, the saint seems certainly to be reflecting. And plainly enough there is, in his tiny frown, a telling indication that reflection's troublesome.

Earlier, the celebrated *St George* (1417) for the church of Orsanmichele in Florence by Donato di Niccolò di Betto Bardi, better known as Donatello, added its own comment on the relationship between wondering and worry, reflection and concern. St George— the original statue is now in the Bargello, Florence—is no muscular hero for Donatello. He's a man of mind. He is not depicted fighting the dragon, as so frequently, but contemplating how to do it. Unlike Restout's Hector, St George is not searching the skies for a clue, either. He's looking at the problem from the level of the earth. He is, for Donatello, an emblem of the Renaissance's privileging of the human mind over supposedly unquestioning faith. He's not Michelangelo's muscle-bound David, glorying in physical form, because St George's principal attribute is his thought. This man will defeat the dragon not only with a spear but with an idea. And Donatello knows that's no easy matter. The saint wonders what, exactly, will happen. Which is the route that will lead to success? How best to kill that dragon? St George, frowning, is as bothered as Aeneas in his journey from the lost Troy to the new and risky world of Rome.

We don't seem to have a clear way of distinguishing in art between thinking and dilemma. If the saint is confident of the will of God then he is also wondering how he is going to bring God's will about, disturbed by his task at the same time. St George isn't serenely assured like the St George of Vittore Carpaccio (c. 1465–1525/6) in the Scuola Grande di San Giorgio degli Schiavoni in Venice. Carpaccio's St George there looks charmingly unruffled by the fierce dragon he is about to strike amid a field of chewed and decaying bodies. Donatello's St George is not like the tranquil saints of Giovanni Bellini (c. 1430–1516), either, who belong in the harmonious world of golden sunlight, the sweet strains of unheard music, the structural balance of shape and color.

Those are figures of secure faith, perhaps—of the worry-free. But Donatello perceives something different about the predicament of being a human being. He was absorbed by the idea of penitence (as his *Mary Magdalene* in the Museo dell' Opera del Duomo in Florence arrestingly indicates). Donatello cared about regret for mistaken decisions. His St George clearly hopes not to be repentant later.

Much of our history, our cultural narratives, celebrates the birth of reason, of men and women as thinking beings, despite the warnings of Genesis. Yet reason hasn't proved only a cause for joy. "Homo sapiens" means "wise man" but was it a wholly wise decision to apply it to us? The worrier knows well that reason can identify the options and evaluate them. Reason can gather information. It can enumerate the issues. It can search out matters pertinent to the problem in hand. But the worrier's reason is notoriously bad at suggesting a way forward. The worrier is acutely aware of reason's capacity to undo the supposedly clarifying work of reason itself. We worriers are good at fretting about what to do next, precisely with the help of reason. The birth of thinking power is the birth of worry in part because thinking allows the worrier to assess alternatives, to try to take everything into account, to muse on what to do about an uncertain future, without being able to decide. We can think for ourselves rather than blindly trust? We can make up our minds? We are free to decide what to do next? Yet the worrier has privileged access to the disappointing realization that our tools aren't up to the task.

The mysterious figure of the ancient Greek philosopher Socrates (c. 469 BC–399 BC) is credited with the Socratic mode of teaching. This is the now familiar question-and-answer mode of writing philosophy where the philosopher invents a scene of tutelage between a teacher and pupil. The questions that are posed in the dialogue are designed to elicit comprehensive answers so that, gradually, an argument—ideally—is articulated; a philosophical position is described, justified, and defended. Much used by Socrates's pupil Plato, the dialogue form has helped implant a strong sense in philosophical discussion (rightly or wrongly) that, in matters of the mind, there *are* answers to questions. Inquiries about philosophical conundrums, about ethics, politics, aesthetics, and even on the grandest topics of the nature and purpose of life, can be posed to a figure of authority, a thinker, who will be able to reply. Socrates has left us, at the most general level, with a certainty that hard questions have answers. But the worrier has translated the Socratic method into his or her own mind. We ask questions within and of ourselves—and, often or not, no-one responds.

The worrier's perturbed not only by the consequences of inhabiting a world of choice but by a powerful and guilty sense that thinking—as in at least a popular understanding of the Socratic method—is supposed to make things plainer. He or she may be troubled by the conviction that, crudely expressed, the legacy of the Enlightenment is about enlightenment, about shining the light of the mind on matters of uncertainty so that they're clearer. Yet decisions can be paralyzed because worriers think over the different alternatives and understand in luminous detail that each course of action has difficulties of its own. We uniquely understand that the more you think the *less* clear matters become. Worry's a kind of mental risk assessment that regularly fails to result in an action plan ("risk assessment," by the way, is a term first recorded in 1957 in the United States, deep into the Age of Worry; "action plan" comes from nearer its beginning, in 1889). Should I apply for this job? What would it be like if I bought a house here? Is this car better than that car? Should I go by train or drive? Is there *actually* something wrong with that cat? Should I take an umbrella to work this morning? Is it the right thing to ask her to dinner?

I'm not sure.

Then there's the self-rebuking when the risk assessment identifies a risk—I might leave my mobile phone at home when I go away for three days—and then, as the Health and Safety people, the Bankers and the Investment brokers say, I fail to "manage the risk." I fail to steer clear of the problem and walk straight into the thing I was trying to avoid. Oh, what dismal little episodes of self-rebuke are here! The worrier's internal self-censorship when he gets to Platform 3 and finds—*horror*—that he *has* left his mobile phone on the bedside table, despite having dutifully packed the charger, and, worse, despite all the worry about leaving the phone; despite all the little reminders and the reassurances to himself that he would remember it. (The worries that gather around communication technology are peculiarly intense because, no doubt, such technology is bound up with reassurance, with things that promise security and connection.) To look into the worrier's mind in the next few minutes, there on Platform 3, would be like looking through a grille into a torture chamber. With this kind of self-criticism, this self-admonishment, which worrier needs someone else to point out their mistakes?

It's easy to celebrate the ability to work things out for ourselves. But what if we can't work things out? We're encouraged to believe in the notion that there's a "right decision" but that hardly helps our state of mind. Such a belief nourishes guilt, inadequacy, frustration, and overwork. And we have readily turned the idea of the "right decision" into a fetish. Our professional lives, certainly, are dominated by managers' beliefs in the right decision—sometimes our ordinary, domestic lives can be too. Here's a problem, the manager says—and what is the right decision, the right solution, the thing that will improve matters? What is your *action plan*? What are your initiatives to make sure that *this* happens and *that* does not? What are the right proposals, going forward? There may be better decisions and worse decisions. There may be compromises that work better than others; there may be solutions that make a greater number of people happier than others. But when does the "right decision," when does any decision about an important matter, come unaccompanied by difficulties of its own?

The dream of reason's work as a bringer of harmonious progression is a vision that's hard to live with. We're daily confronted with the assumption that there are ideal solutions, that there are responses and decisions that take everything important into account and that there are ways ahead where everyone is happy. The dream of reason's work is nowhere clearer in recent times than in the writing of the English philosopher and Utilitarian, John Stuart Mill. Mill's an inspiring thinker about the progress that reason, and free and frank discussion, can supposedly bring. He's the champion, particularly in his famous treatise *On Liberty* (1859), of a liberal society, of the free press, of academic freedom, of the democratic, of the values of intellectual liberty. All this is good. But Mill is also a great stick with which worriers can beat themselves up.

On Liberty proposes the liberal dream that free and candid discussion, the unencumbered play of the reasoning mind, will sort things out. He has a noble faith in the idea that rational thought will liberate truths and that discussion between those who disagree will really be a progression toward consensus as each side attends to what is right in the other's views. "As mankind improve[s]," Mill says, with enormous, perilous confidence in such advancement, "the number of doctrines which are no longer disputed or doubted will be constantly on the increase: and the well-being of mankind may almost be measured by the number and gravity of the truths which have reached the point of being uncontested."[8] And they'll have reached that point not by the assertive will of mere authority but by conversation.

---

[8] *The Collected Works of John Stuart Mill*, ed. by J. M. Robson, 33 vols (Toronto: University of Toronto Press, 1963–1991), xviii.250.

Mill's concerned not to fetter the expression of any opinion so long as it is expressed temperately. For him, silencing any view is always an act that weakens the chance of the full truth being understood. He summarizes his case as follows:

First, if any opinion is compelled to silence, that opinion may, for aught we can certainly know, be true. To deny this is to assume our own infallibility.

Secondly, though the silenced opinion be an error, it may, and very commonly does, contain a portion of truth; and since the general or prevailing opinion on any object is rarely or never the whole truth, it is only by the collision of adverse opinions that the remainder of the truth has any chance of being supplied.

Thirdly, even if the received opinion be not only true, but the whole truth; unless it is suffered to be, and actually is, vigorously and earnestly contested, it will, by most of those who receive it, be held in the manner of a prejudice, with little comprehension or feeling of its rational grounds. And not only this, but, fourthly, the meaning of the doctrine itself will be in danger of being lost, or enfeebled, and deprived of its vital effect on the character and conduct: the dogma becoming a mere formal profession, inefficacious for good, but cumbering the ground, and preventing the growth of any real and heartfelt conviction, from reason or personal experience.[9]

What lies behind this is a sturdy, an almost incredible, belief in human progress through the wonder of the reasoning mind. Free discussion of opposing views will, naturally, result in agreement, in movement toward consent. And what's generally agreed is, in Mill's terms, truthful. (Mill doesn't worry himself that discussions might

---

[9]Ibid., p. 258.

result in agreement on mistaken things. He's not bothered by what to me is a familiar spectacle: a large group of people deciding, after much apparently rational thought, on the wrong course of action.) Truth is, supposedly, steadily freed and eventually it will even become necessary, in Mill's idea of the progressing world, to imagine that an established truth has not yet been agreed and to debate it anyway so as to keep it "alive." The Socratic method, as it happens, will do perfectly well in Mill's conception as a way of preserving the vitality of an established truth.

Reason as a way of liberating truth; as a guide to decision-making; as a light by which to walk; as a way of bringing disparate and unharmonious views into harmony: Mill's *On Liberty* sketches an audacious progress narrative on the back of the truth-exposing power of thought. At the center of human history and its progress is neither a book nor an altar but a seminar. Yet the worrier just can't see it like this. If Mill's ideas of free discussion, of the democratic nature of civilized life, of the limits of state to dictate to us, of the limits of mere authority to control us, are among the foundations of the modern West, then they are also the ideas that help the worrier to worry.

The liberal dream is of society's gradual advance through open discussion where everything is tolerated except intolerance; where everything is discussed in the belief that rightness, released by thought, will eventually prevail. But the worrier knows all too well that reason, trying to evaluate options, isn't a reliable guide to certainty or agreement. It's not safe. If reason *could* reply to worry, and reach a consensus as to what was true or right or best, then there wouldn't be a problem. We would have replaced the Gods with a form of thinking that *was* able to take everything into account, was able to reach "the right decision," which Mill bracingly calls the "truth." Worry, haunted by Mill's assertion that "Wrong opinions and practices gradually yield to fact and argument,"[10] uses reason to demonstrate with dismaying lucidity how many possibilities, difficulties, and issues there are in any one matter. Worry erodes confidence in the "right answer" by rationally analyzing the implications of decisions, and, often enough, paralyzing choice in well-informed, well-argued, impressively analyzed indecision.

The worrier knows that the expression of the contrary opinions doesn't always lead to greater clarity, let alone accord. The worrier knows that such opinions, as they are generated in his or her mind, will distract and confuse. The worrier knows too, as he or she implicitly provides a critique of the principles of intellectual liberalism, that continually thinking about things does not result in unambiguous ways ahead. Mill's progress narrative taunts the worrier, bogged down in the painful assessment and reassessment of what he or she should do or think. The notion that every idea, every perspective and proposition, should be contested, or at least be free to be contested, is hardly for worriers anything like an ideal situation. It's all too close to the world we live in anyway.

It's hard not to forget, in turn, the fate of periodicals who ventured on similar principles to Mill's. George Henry Lewes (1817–78), polymathic British writer and in due course the partner of George Eliot, launched *The Leader* in 1850. That was a periodical distinguished from other mid-century journals by its belief in free speech (no anonymous writing here, no hiding behind the abstract authority of a journal's name). *The Leader*'s faith in free speech, the open avowal of opinions on all matters untrammeled by convention or propriety, wasn't a result simply of its editor's dislike of censorship. The founders of *The Leader* believed that rational debate would reach conclusions that would be generally acceptable and generally true. This was *On Liberty* before *On Liberty*.

---

[10]Ibid., p. 231.

A particular feature of *The Leader* was a section called "Open Council" where correspondence was invited on any topic and "wherein *every* Opinion may find a voice."[11] But "Open Council" quickly went off-message. First, correspondents wrote at too great a length and in a tedious fashion; then they were personally affronting to other authors and to the editors of the journal itself. And then the novelist and clergyman Charles Kingsley (1819–75), author of *The Water-Babies* (1863), wrote to denounce *The Leader* in its entirety. Far from contributing to the "emancipation of truth,"[12] as the "Open Council" had originally intended, the feature gave public room to disagreement, denunciation, and embarrassing failure to reach anything even like a compromise let alone a consensus. A worrier—fretful of the future and doubtful of where too much thinking will lead us—would have predicted that.

J. S. Mill was confident that "liberating" the "truth" would occur through well-mannered debate, the exercise of a grown-up human being's capacity to reason. He was also, it seems, confident that the "truth" would be liberating. The "*well-being* of mankind," he says, "may almost be measured by the number and gravity of the truths which have reached the point of being uncontested." Here was another side of the liberal dream: rational thought on all matters of human interest will identify truths that will be beneficial to all; that will enhance human *well-being*. The worrier doubts that too. We are far more likely to think of truths, of knowledge or certainty, as something that will do nothing of the sort. Truth is not axiomatically beauty; truth is not axiomatically conducive to well-being. Reason, endeavoring to take all things into account, struggles to reach conclusions that are simply reassuring or which simply contribute to the growth of

---

[11] *The Leader*, 1 (1850), p. 12.
[12] Ibid.

happiness. Reason's task in the worrier's mind is to discern pathways to difficulties, problems, wrinkles. Even at the most ordinary levels we know this. "If I took this job then I would be leaving a secure position for a riskier one . . ." "If this pain in my leg is arthritis, then it may stop me walking so easily . . ."; "If I left my keys in the car, it could be stolen . . ." And beyond these local troubles and all their kin are the gravest matters. How much of what Mill cheerfully calls the "truth" *really* contributes to our well-being? How much of what reason tells us is "true" can we tolerate?

Among the root causes of worry in an individual's mind is, it may be, an entrenched insecurity. Certainly, it's the precariousness and chanciness of the world in which we live that helps produce fretting. But, for the moment, it's not merely the chanciness of the broadest environment that I want to take into account but, briefly, the internal mental and emotional security of the person who must manage it, must negotiate his or her way through that environment. Worry enters edifices that don't look too stable. Worry makes of unfixed foundations its best home. The uncertain individual—uncertain in mind or in feelings—is in turn worry's natural prey. Worry is focused on an uncertainty about the future—"*what if . . .?*"—and that future looks even more troubling from a perspective that isn't itself secure.

There are many powerful reasons for such individual insecurity and no doubt Freud and psychoanalysts would tell us more. Perhaps what the worrier doesn't want to think about, privately, is the rootlessness of his or her own inner life; its lack of anchor in certainty or purpose. Others, Freudians included, might be keen to look to past traumas, separation anxieties, repressed memories. We all might muse, for instance, on the classic psychological experiment of the "unlicked rat." This is an experiment (not by any means the worst in the history of science's relationship with nonhuman animals) with parent rats and their offspring (kittens in Great Britain, pups in the United States). It involves a researcher handling some, but not all, of the baby rats for a few minutes several times a day. The outcome of this experiment is that the rats that have been handled by humans are, when adults, more inquisitive, confident, and determined. They're larger and bolder. The rats that are not handled will often be more timid, less well grown, more nervous. These are less confident, less sure in responding to their environment, and less able to adapt to change and new things. How could this be? How could being handled by a *human being* be good for a baby rat?

The answer seems to be that, on being returned to the family, the baby rat that has been handled by a human being is vigorously washed by the adult rats. The baby has arrived with the scent of an alien and so is cleaned up each time. But the key thing is that licking is also the chief expression, for a rat, of care. Being touched by human beings is a trigger that prompts extended attention. It seems tempting to say that this handling of the baby rat encourages the expression of love.

The experiment is, in one way, oppressively ideological. But it certainly appears to suggest an influential way in which a lack of confidence may come into human life or into lives more generally. Certainly, a Freudian reading of the meaning of worry might see it as arising from the loss of the womb, an effect of the primary trauma of losing the bonds of infancy. We have got some powerful ideas about how to locate the personal causes of worry though, to be honest, I'm not sure yet whether I understand, or quite believe, any of them in my concern to identify the external more than the private factors that shape my worrying. I'm more interested in the ample, the more extended, the contextual. I'm more bothered by things that can be said about the insecurity not of each individual but of us all. I'm suspicious, that is, of Mill's liberal hope that truths contribute to "well-being"—because, simply, we *are* insecure.

I don't mean that we are psychologically insecure. I mean the grand and shocking truths, as well as the sordid, dark, and miserable ones, which Mill's cheerful and actually deeply theological vision of life can't or won't accommodate. (When I say theological, I mean that he believes profoundly in order, in the perfectibility of human society and our ability to achieve collective harmony.) We live with precariousness, violence, and trouble on a scale that's hard to imagine. The catastrophic histories retold in, say, W. G. Sebald's *The Rings of Saturn* (1995) and the bleak calamities recuperated in Stefan Chwin's *Death in Danzig* (1995) are only the most recent literary narratives I've reread that provide not merely a factual but also an imaginative connection with the shock of human history. Here are forms of torment, truths about how we behave, that reason can't convert into well-being. Worry may be a defense mechanism against daily troubles, a kind of safeguard against our regular exposure to risk. But, for the most part, that's only the smallest pointer to the real dangers that beset us and the real condition of our lives, lived perilously on an overexploited planet with a finite life span, where death will catch up with us in the end. To safeguard against *these* conditions, to hide them with an assertion that truth always intensifies well-being, is absurd.

The end point of reason isn't as Mill would have it. The end point is to realize, at our grimmest, the unconsoled ridiculousness of human life. Looked at like that, from a secular and materialist viewpoint, it's hard to see the contentment allegedly brought by Mill's hope in the truth of things, the things of truth. We're better off, we are happier, with myths and fictions; we're better off with thinking about what isn't the case. Looked at from this perspective, the worrier is peculiarly able to apprehend that well-being resides in disguises and misreadings, not in fully faced actuality. We're the new visionaries of the modern world, the new poets and prophets. We can see a different and contrary verity to Mill: we know that human beings are happier with lies.

Considering *On Liberty* and its implications makes me realize, too, one of the stranger and smaller advantages of ordinary, daily, domestic worry. Although the end point of thinking might well be something horrible, common or garden worry keeps us focused on what's actually more manageable. It keeps us focused on the common or garden. Regular, day-to-day worry concerns matters where, often enough, we *do* have some control, some chance of making things work out, of avoiding the worst case scenario of "*what if . . .?*" Ordinary worry usually keeps me, certainly, absorbed with the local and—so it now might seem—at least partially controllable. Ordinary worry pulls me back to the micro-level of my own life and to "little" decisions. I have *some* influence on those. Here is something paradoxically reassuring about worry: it's usually so parochial, so pleasingly concerned with minutiae. We *can* decide—if we really make an effort—to apply or not to apply for a job, however much we worry about it; we can decide to buy this car or that; we can decide that it might be better to see a doctor about that toe after all. These might be difficult or even bad decisions. But we can at least, in the little world of our daily living, make them. Worry need not, for the most part, be *entire* paralysis. And even if it is, worry still keeps us focused on the common not the cosmic. Worry refers us, often enough, to matters about which we *can* do something so long as we can bring ourselves to act. Worry, the fretful evaluation of the options in our life, might seem to distract us from the business of living happily. But it also distracts us—in our consuming anxieties about the quotidian, the humdrum—from troubles that dwarf our ordinary concerns. Ordinary worries are, looked at like this, counterintuitively, a kind of blessing. "Present fears | Are less than horrible imaginings,"[13] says Macbeth. He's right.

---

[13]*Macbeth*, 1:3:136–7.

Worry begins with the capacity to think, the very defining faculty of human consciousness in the deepest narratives of our culture. In turn, worry generates anxieties by identifying problems with every next step and problematizes decision as it problematizes happiness. One of the things that Pandora let out of her box, most definitely, was thought. The very definition of a free human being is, we have now come to accept, not only the ability but the right to think for oneself. That's part of the most significant intellectual and ethical definition of what "freedom" now means. It's the ground of democracy, of our optimism for human society. Yet more recently the celebrated freedom of the individual, as a political objective and an intellectual one, has become economic. Freedom has been best expressed in another term whose heritage stretches back, once again, to the birth of independent thought: choice.

Choice comes into being as soon as the omnipotent and tyrannical Gods have gone. As soon as men and women have no absolute power ruling them, they're free from the prison-house and out among possibilities, decisions, and dilemmas. The existence of choice is a flag of freedom, even if Genesis declares it as the deadly result of sin, and choosing is now, more than ever, what we need to set our minds to. Like Adam and Eve departing the gates of Eden, we can certainly select where to go: "The world," as Milton said, "was all before them, where to choose | Their place of rest."[14] But far beyond choosing merely the place of rest (assuming for a moment there is such a place), the contemporary marketplace advises us that we can choose pretty much everything. It's no longer sin or the result of sin. It's liberty and success. Yet the privileging of choice in the politics and economics of the contemporary world challenges the worrier's life yet more.

---

[14]John Milton, *Paradise Lost*, ed. Alastair Fowler, 2nd edn (Harlow: Longman, 1997), Book XII, ll.648–9.

The privileging of choice is a natural corollary of free market economics that champions open competition as the driver of prosperity and, beyond that, as the supposed guarantor of quality or its modern replacement: "value-for-money." The fact that I have a choice of coffee to buy energizes, in theory, the coffee sellers to offer better quality, better service, and better "value for money." The idea of the free market has become entangled with the conception that human life will flourish in every sense if each individual is "freed" not only to think for themselves but to compete against everyone else without hindrance except that of law. In turn, the free market has become the economic basis for a faith in the "right" of individuals to act according to their own independent decisions, to choose freely. We're encouraged to share a conviction that we have a "right" to live our own lifestyles and to have our thoughts and feelings taken into account. Far more dimly, we're invited to believe that, improving our own position, we're contributing to the collective good in the process. Although the notion of choice, particularly in economics, hardly dares contemplate the larger question of the collective good, the unspoken assumption remains, fuzzily, that such a good must be somehow achieved by our own individual fulfillment. In choosing for ourselves, in getting what we want, we're apparently doing everyone a service.

Having choice is now the necessary part of a politics of human liberty. Even if, in England, we'd rather have one hospital that offers high quality care, we are invited to value the presence of choice—we can select between several hospitals with mixed reports of quality— because such choice affirms us as individual exercisers *of* choice; as people who can express our own preferences; as people who can have what suits us best. The extent of an individual's choice is not only, crucially, an indication of the flourishing of the market and of the success of "freedom" as an economic principle, but of the prosperity and success of the chooser. If a man or woman has the resources to choose any of the options available then he or she has obtained the highest point of success in that particular market (this cookie or that; this hotel or that; these state-run schools or these independent ones; this state health care or that private hospital; this yacht or that private luxury submarine). Choice marks individual freedom just as it is the agent for the display of individual achievement.

Yet choice is hard to handle! Even the literal market stalls that display 40 different kinds of handmade soap, or 60 different kinds of candles, are little scenes of trouble.[15] How to decide? Is loganberry and whiskey mousse really a nicer taste than blackberry on its own? Is this strawberry yoghurt better or worse for having only fruit sugar in it? The literal marketplace, when it's apparently overwhelmed with choice, may well result in fewer sales; may well result in the consumer's confusion. We might well hope, in the literal marketplace, to choose, but only to a point. Too much choice paralyzes choosing—even for the nonworrier. Selecting between 6 cakes rather than 60 is an easier proposition. One of the decent reasons for being a vegetarian (there are better ones) is that it reduces the epic struggle of menu reading. Which of these starters will make me happiest? Which main course should I have (and how much will I regret not having another if I do?). Ah, no, I am a vegetarian: the goat's cheese and red onion tart, please. What a relief.

The pressure that's building around the implications of the "right to choose" in capitalist societies throws fuel into the engine room of

---

[15]There is some recent consideration of the paralysis of choice in Alena Tugend's 2010 *New York Times* article, "Too many choices: A Problem that Can Paralyze" (see http://www.nytimes.com/2010/02/27/your-money/27shortcuts.html?_r=0, last accessed February 4, 2014). The classic jam study is discussed in Sheena Iyengar's valuable book, *The Art of Choosing* (New York: Twelve, 2010). There is a bracing analysis of the modern world's love affair with an illusory choice in Kent Greenfield's *The Myth of Choice: Personal Responsibility in a World of Limits* (New Haven, CT: Yale University Press, 2011).

worry, stoking up the heat produced by the implications of the more basic fact that it's thinking that defines us as human beings. Wouldn't it be easier if quality could be guaranteed in some other way (assuming for a moment that quality *is* guaranteed by the free market)? Parents endeavor to work out whether this school or that is better for their child; patients, in the United Kingdom at any rate, are offered the choice between this hospital and that. The temptation to stay with the local school or the closest hospital is real. There's relief in having a smaller choice even if, intellectually, we may want to choose the best we can afford. And the amount of data—the league tables, the brochures, the inspectors' reports, the financial statements—doesn't always help, and not because the information is sparse or inaccessible but because it's apparently full and in the public domain. The wealth of information intensifies the difficulty about decisions. If only interpreting league tables were a straightforward matter, says the fretful parent or the patient. If only we had the inside knowledge to understand really what these figures, this metric, that metric, mean. (And anyway, isn't it the case—the worrier might be the first to notice—that league tables force perverse behaviors? Don't they encourage organizations to prioritize behavior that pushes them higher in the tables, even if there is no close correlation between the behavior and actual quality?) Being made to choose is hard work.

Modern capitalism increases choice (or at least it *says* it does) and to increase the data on which choices should be made. The political right celebrates choice even more fervently as the sign of "liberty," an apparently inalienable entitlement. But things don't get any better for our mental well-being when the business of choosing develops further into the logical corollary that failure is the individual's fault. If my daughter isn't happy at school that's because I didn't pay enough attention to all those reports and chose badly. Or perhaps it's because I didn't get out to night-school when I was younger and improve my qualifications, and therefore my job, and therefore my income, and therefore the kind of school I could send my daughter to. If the man who repaired my back door did it badly, that's because I have chosen him lazily and without enough research. Or maybe it's because I failed to get a better job to allow me to pay for a better tradesman? We've only ourselves to blame if we're not any good at choosing or haven't the resources to choose. Failure, here, comes as an individual's mistake, a misjudgment. It's remarkable what this theory of the market, the ideology of choice, is doing to us.

The cosmetic surgery industry advises us that we can choose what we look like.[16] The postmodern world of flexible identity even means that we can choose different personae, even a different sex or ethnicity. We can *choose* to be male or female; black or white; taller or shorter; with a smaller nose or not. The internet chat room allows us space to define new roles and new identities to perform in a virtual world. We can pretend to be someone completely different—not for suspicious or criminal purposes but because it's fun and allows us to explore a new part of our identity. These are not, as little of what I'm describing about the modern world of choice, *inherently* bad things. In all sorts of ways, they are things to celebrate. It's just that they have the awkward side effect of raising the temperature of worrying yet again. The adverts tell us we can choose this lifestyle or that if we buy this product or that. We can be who we want to be, look how we want to look. We can choose a product but we can also choose to believe in the lifestyle with which it is associated: we can choose to buy a new way of existing, however illusory. It's even ironically the case that insurance advertisements, I've noticed, play expertly with the very terms that the free market and the breathless world of choice

---

[16]There is a full account of what, exactly, we're now permitted to choose in Renata Salecl's *Choice* (London: Profile, 2010).

are making harder to obtain. The adverts tell us that in purchasing insurance we'll buy "peace of mind." Being worry-free is a commodity too! And, like every other purchase, it's really our fault if we haven't enough money, or will, to buy it.

Even harder to resist—and equally guilt-inducing—is the embedding of this rhetoric of choice, and its "management," in our professional lives. It's harder to resist simply because if we don't accept it, we get into trouble and we might get fired. It's true that Human Resources (HR) or Personnel departments in modern businesses have, in a variety of ways, taken over the work that used to be undertaken in the United Kingdom by trades unions. HR attends to contracts. They monitor us to make sure that there's no discrimination in selection processes; that men and women are paid the same; that those on fixed-term contracts receive the same support as those on open-ended contracts; that bullying in the workplace is tackled. This is valuable. It's necessary. But HR has now little distance from the managers, from the idea of making a workforce conform. And the assumptions of modern management are, increasingly, to encourage us to think that our success at work is primarily a matter of choice.

Apparently, we can *choose* to improve our skills as leaders and negotiators by attending this course or that. We can choose to manage our time better if we go on another course about—time management. We can, in my world, apparently choose to teach better, or write better books, if only we're willing. The key issue is not capacity but decision; not ability but will. HR can advise us that we should be trained in this; that we should "develop skills" in that. We can choose to improve. We can even go to anger management classes if things get really bad: apparently, we can choose whether to be annoyed at work or not. Our personality as well as our capacities and abilities are not of primary relevance for they can be shaped by will. This is the immense modern extension of "freedom" into the workplace—an extension that has turned freedom into a species of coercion.

The proliferating workplace discourse of "well-being" is a discourse of choice, too. We may think that centuries of philosophy, literature, and art have struggled to articulate the toughest questions of what makes human beings happy or good. But, in some comical ways, HR reassures us that they have the answers. We can choose. We can decide to develop tools, through more courses, that enable us to "manage" how we feel.

This is a strange, perverse, outcome of the discourses of "liberty." And wrapped up with this conception of choice is another contemporary form of moral reprobation. For, in this discourse of choice, it follows once more that we ourselves are at fault if things go wrong. The language of choice implies at work, as in choosing schools for our children or buying dinner in a restaurant, that we've ourselves to blame, in part or in whole, if we're not happy or not successful. We've made learning errors; we didn't attend to the class. We misjudged or didn't properly understand. We made the wrong decision. Darian Leader puts this well when thinking about the culture of cognitive behavior therapy, the therapeutic side of the notion that we choose who and what we are. CBT, he says in *The New Black: Mourning, Melancholia and Depression* (2008), "sees people's symptoms as the outcome of faulty learning. With proper re-education, they can correct their behaviour and bring it closer to the desired norm."[17] It's difficult to resist the logic of that conclusion. We can train ourselves to be happy just as, at work, we can be trained not to find the arrogant, self-centered behavior of some of those we work with, even mildly irritating. Our fundamental error where misery or depression is concerned, or the

---

[17]Darian Leader, *The New Black: Mourning, Melancholia and Depression* (2008, London: Penguin, 2009), p. 18.

root cause of any sorrow or trouble or pain or worry, is that we didn't decide differently.

Worry about what to choose and worry about the guilt involved in choosing wrongly: the "freedom" of the human being to think and to decide makes life for the modern worrier rough. We worriers are a modest but still a real litmus test of exactly what we're doing to ourselves. Given the overwhelming presence of choice in our culture, by the way, it's noticeable how vigorously one area of our lives is still constructed as dominated by fate and not by choice. It is as if the language of destiny, of the all-knowing Gods, has been forced back into aggressive and intimidating use because it's been squeezed out everywhere else. I mean romance, the language of love. "The One" is the regular term of magazines and journals, of films and newspapers, for the perfect soul mate who's out there waiting for the singleton to discover them: "is he The One?" parents and friends inquire of their daughters, hoping she is finally going to tie the knot. This is the new "when-are-you-going-to-get-settled?" ritual. In the old days, parents used to ask about the prospective partner's income, prospects, family connections. Now, they're more likely to fall headlong for the language of the magazines. Is she the One? Is he the One? It's hard to avoid the attraction of this momentous inquiry. "Destiny" plays a conspicuous role in so many popular narrations of whom we decide to share our lives with: "across a crowded room . . . And somehow you know." Choice is only a matter, here, of acceding to the will of Cupid who continues busily to flit around popular conceptions of how we make romantic choices, persuading us that there's only one person in the world with whom we could be properly happy. Only one person—though we happened to meet them at work, or in a bar in Seattle while waiting for someone else, or accidentally at a bus stop. Fate fights back in that fretful world of choice. But actually it still doesn't make things much better. All we have to worry about now is that we have understood what fate is telling us—oh yeah, and that fate has got it right.

The language of choice, of personal responsibility, can reach long distances. William Glasser's *Choice Theory: A New Psychology of Personal Freedom* (1998) takes, as I see it, the free market as far as it could go in relation to individual identity. At least, I *hope* this is as far as it can go. *Choice Theory* is a self-help book that brings us to the last frontier of the crossover between the language of choice, the discourse of "liberty," and the sources of human happiness. And ironically enough it's a book about worrying that uses the very terms, the very conditions and assumptions, which makes worry our contemporary. The language of freedom, choice, decision, and the power of reasoning are, here, boldly, even aggressively, turned against one of the things they have collectively helped to bring into the world.

Choice, for Dr Glasser, is the key to our romantic lives, to all our relationships, to our happiness altogether. It really is the fundamental matter that determines who and what we are. Choice is, certainly, the answer to worriers. We're born into a world where we learn immediately that we can control our parents by crying, Glasser observes. And we have to spend the rest of our lives unlearning that desire to control others. We have to recognize the right of others to choose, and, more consequentially, we have to stop believing that our own happiness, or our sense of self-worth, is dependent on others doing as we say. We also, ourselves, have to realize that directly or indirectly we choose who we are, how we feel, who we are with, and what our future is. It's down to us individually—and it's down to our individual control over our individual selves, not over others.

This discrimination between freedoms, where each person is, apparently, free to be just who they wish to be without conflicting with the desires of others, develops into the boldest account of just how much authority we have over who we are. *Choice Theory* concerns mental health. If we're depressed about the breakup of a relationship, for instance, then that, in this energetic transference of the free market into feelings, is an act of choice. Dr Glasser creates an ungainly verb: we choose "to depress." The verb-from-noun emphasizes the active selection of unhappiness. "[Few] of us are prepared to recognize that something is seriously wrong with our lives," he observes, contentiously: "It is more comfortable to blame our discomfort on a mental illness."[18] But what's really happening is the *personal* decision "to depress." However, thought-provoking this idea is—that our response is our responsibility—it comes with a well-developed rhetoric of blame. It's an extreme point of the new choice-culture's language of sin that we worriers could particularly do without.

The essence of "choice theory," says Glasser, lies in the use of verbs to describe what we've chosen ("to depress" is the perfect example). Verbs exemplify the theory, he declares, because they make something active and create a doer—they imply that a noun is really a willed selection, something to inhabit and live by. Beyond that, the verbs require a subject, someone who is doing the action; someone who confirms choice theory's basic proposition that we decide how we feel and we decide what happens to us. What our mental state is like, how we suffer and how we react, are selections. The privileging of the verbs—especially "to depress"—affirms what a demanding world Choice Theory describes. It's one where we can't hide even behind grammar to claim that something is outside us and happens to us— like depression. We decided to be depressed—we decided to worry.

It's tough indeed. Does the rape survivor whose life is shattered by violation really only have herself or himself to blame for unhappiness afterward, for *deciding* on depression after the rape? It's hard to admit,

---

[18]William Glasser, M. D., *Choice Theory: A New Psychology of Personal Freedom* (New York: HarperCollins, 1999), p. 86.

in this theory, even the most obvious truths that some things are overwhelming, that they take away choice because they belong to a world where our own agency is torn apart and where we can't choose how we respond because we have no control over what's happening to us. The "tough, responsible" world of Choice Theory desires to empower, to persuade us that happiness, despite everything, lies in our own hands. We can grasp it or refuse it, apparently—whatever happens.

An antagonist of Behaviorism, Glasser urges us to believe that we choose our lives as far as our genes allow. That's the only inhibitor he admits. This is, in fact, a kind of extreme expression of the political right, the championing of human liberty and the right of self-determination, in mental health. We must be free and responsible for ourselves and, since nothing stands in our way except for genes, then nothing can be blamed on anyone else other than our own decisions. If I fail, I (and you) know exactly whom to blame. If I succeed, I deserve (as I trust you'll appreciate) all the credit. And if having choice is, in modern capitalism, a source of bewilderment and anxiety, it is in Choice Theory the fertile ground of sterner self-rebuke, self-criticism, self-blame. "Not only did I find making this decision difficult, and not only must I repudiate myself for any failure of that decision to be successful or to bring happiness, I must expect everyone else to understand that I am the author of my own unhappiness. I have chosen where I am, how I feel, and what my life is like."

The powerful allure of a belief in personal "liberty," the notion that human beings can be free from everything but their genes to determine their lives, is a tenacious political assumption of our advanced capitalism. It's rooted in a sense of a natural order that is as coherent and planned as any described by the Natural Theology of the eighteenth and early nineteenth centuries. This conception of the central importance of an individual's freedom to follow their own choices, usually, adopts the assumption—however infrequently mentioned—that if everyone pursued those freely made decisions, all would be well. The complete expression of individual freedoms as the ground of human culture rests on the belief—which can never be tested just as it is rarely discussed—that there's still some kind of mystical or God-given order for the human species. Such order means that the maximum success and happiness of the world will be obtained when all men and women have as much freedom as their genes will allow and are able to act according to their own individual desires, choices, needs. In the wonderful future, so envisaged, there may only appear to be individuals choosing, individuals following the logic of what they individually want. But there will also be a coherent and secure global society too. That's an audacious, boldly expanded version of John Stuart Mill's conviction in the middle of the nineteenth century that if we could all think and discuss freely then the general well-being of the world would increase.

If the worrier doubts all of this, sees it from inside his or her own bothered mind, then the worrier may also find the solutions as much of a problem as the causes. No worrier that I know would like to deprive us of the freedom to think for ourselves where we can; of the freedom to decide for ourselves where we can. If we're particularly conscious of the problems of deciding, of having a reasoning mind, we can hardly think the answer to the pain of worrying is to take that freedom to decide away. More locally, the political arguments at present about the problems with the language of choice seem insufficient. For the philosopher and sociologist Renata Salecl in her plainly titled *Choice* (2010), the whole business of choosing is a distraction. "In these times of crisis and uncertainty," she writes, in the midst of global financial problems,

> the ideology of positive thinking plays an essential role in masking
> the need to rethink the nature of social inequalities and trying

to find alternatives to the way capitalism has been developing. When individuals are made to feel they are the masters of their own destiny, and when positive thinking is offered as the panacea for the ills that they suffer as the result of social injustice, social critique is increasingly replaced by self-critique.[19]

That's obviously the argument of the Left to the Right; the thinker who considers society versus the thinker who prioritizes the individual; the person who looks at structures that inhibit versus the person who concentrates on individual accountability for personal destiny; the writer who privileges collective responsibility versus the writer who privileges individual choice. Salecl's objections, reasonably enough, are to the occluding work that the language of choice does. Such language, she thinks, encourages us to believe simply that we're responsible for all the problems that exist in our world. And, whatever other issues this involves, the celebration of choice is a great inhibitor of structural reform. Choice, in Salecl's argument, focuses everything at such a local level—on the individual's aspirations and desires—that it stops us looking at the larger, more threatening issues: climate change, corruption, global justice, financial peril, poverty, tyranny.

There's truth in that. But the personal costs of choice can't be dismissed. If it's correct that "social critique is increasingly [being] replaced by self-critique" in the extension of choice culture, it's also the case that the self-critique is taking its toll. When a worrier reads a self-help book, hopeful, perhaps, of a cure, it's worth knowing just exactly what it is that has to be "cured" and whether it is actually in our power to choose the alternative.

Worriers would need to do more than change their private beliefs about themselves, or decide to go on a course. We'd need to do more

---

[19]Salecl, *Choice*, p. 31.

than simply trust that things will be better than we fear, and more than merely believe that we could manage our minds and feelings better and get a grip. We worriers would have, it seems, to go a horribly long way back into history and do nothing less than—well—start over again. What evidence we have from the ancient world, the foundational (and not at all ancient) cultures of Western society, implies that it was impossible even to *imagine* what life felt like before thinking. So we really would have to go back to a beginning about which we have no clue. And we'd have to start off along a different track and find some new ways of making decisions and some other ways of defining human beings that didn't depend on reason and the freedom to choose.

Our reasoning mind has come, in the contemporary world, to be bogged down in debilitating conditions of fretful decision-making and persistent blame, the grim and politicized consequences of the apparently innocent and cheering pleasures of choosing. But the incipient problems with reason, and thus the far, far remote dawning of the conditions of worry, were there at the beginning, whenever that was. They were there at the very moment that humanity, back in time irrecoverable, began to think about the world at all.

4

Accept distracted thanks

Troilus and Cressida, 5:2:191

I'm worried that this book shows all the symptoms of a classic worrier. *Worrying* appears to be a reflex of its own gaunt subject. My argument develops, quickly, from a low-level thought about a back door to a description of the grave problems of living in a world of reason and in modern capitalist society. It might be said that this book is dressed about with a sort of enervating fatalism—caught between a desire to be humane and a de-energized sense that, after all, there's little to be done, little real relief, little more to do than moan. *Worrying* has so far considered fretfulness as not merely some minor uncertainty about whether a door is locked or not but, in truth, the cumulative and inescapable result of converging historical forces that are impossible to escape. There is, in this respect, a scale problem that's absurd. Woody Allen catches something of—and laughs wryly at—my logical readiness for extremes, my crazy habit of taking ordinary ideas and queries to their extremes, in *Annie Hall* (1977). It's a comedy about a neurotic who dismantles a relationship through his insecurities and oddities. The sufferer, Alvy Singer, is seen as a child at the beginning of the film declaring to a doctor that there's no point in doing his homework because the universe is expanding and, well, some day, everything will fall apart. Alvy can't conceive of a reason why, under such unpropitious circumstances, he should bother with his school work.

Worrying keeps returning to matters to consider them from different angles. There's something of the worrier in that too. My favorite word is "but." There's indecisiveness here, incipiently. Here's reason brooding on things—and failing to work things out. "Ah, yes, but there is another way of thinking of this . . . Have thought about *this*? Are you sure that's the *only* way of looking at it?" So far, I've found it difficult not to perceive everything as somehow related to an underlying worry, as if worry was the plug through which everything else was draining. James Joyce's reader was implicitly encouraged to see that the language around Leopold Bloom, wandering through Dublin in 1904, revealed Bloom's underlying anxieties. Narrative discourse was quietly shaped by the force field of psychological trouble as worries seeped into, and from, the most random or apparently unrelated of matters. The tug of this book is worrying itself. I keep returning to it: the background music can't, it appears, be changed. Surely, an unworrying reader might observe, it is possible to look at a celebrated Renaissance statue without seeing it as some kind of "birth of worry" emblem? Can't you just think about, well—happier things?

There's always something ready for comedy, as well as exasperation, in worrying. The pain of worry is real and sometimes the most real thing in a worrier's mind. But laughter, if it can hardly relieve it, is, in some ways, potentially part of worry. In Shakespeare's plays, comic devices serve as the starting point of grave and sometimes tragic outcomes. An accidentally dropped handkerchief ought to belong with comedy, with the humor of mistaken identities or misunderstood desires. But in *Othello*, the dropped handkerchief disastrously strikes Othello as evidence of his wife's infidelity. That leads to both their deaths. There's something comic about the repeated action of throwing down of gages in *Richard II*, which appears to make the masculine language of brave commitment into a pantomime, a set of ridiculous gestures. Tragedy and disaster may involve things that look comic or start of *as* comic; and in worry, things that are painful and hard can look funny too. Worry prompts amusement. "Nothing is funnier than unhappiness, I grant you that," says Nell in Samuel Beckett's play *Endgame* (1957, as *Fin de partie*). It's "the most comical thing in the world."[1] Beckett's plays in general exploit the uncomfortable comedy of misery, sometimes to laugh-out-loud funny. Nell's lines refer to comic absurdity, to the readiness of those who're suffering even the most dreadful circumstances to find something amusing to say. But Beckett's also interested in the way suffering is itself on the cusp of comedy; how suffering can look, with only the slightest shift of perspective, amusing.

With worry, it's the bathetic or the ludicrous that, most plainly, make for fun. Comedy has a long tradition of making mountains made out of molehills. To return to Shakespeare, the comic subplot of *Twelfth Night* hangs on the interpretation of a single mischievous letter, apparently declaring that Olivia is in love with the steward Malvolio and asking Malvolio to wear cross-garters with yellow stockings, to smile always in Olivia's presence, and to be rude to the other servants. Mischievously persuaded of the letter's authenticity, Malvolio alters his behavior and his appearance. The audience laughs guiltily. But we can't forget that Malvolio has been incautious: he's been duped by a letter that looks all too clearly like a fake. The narratives that derive from minor misjudgments, the accidental interpretations of insecure evidence, are reminders of the way worry can work too.

Worry readily makes embarrassing mountains out of molehills. The distance between the starting point and the conclusion in the worrier's

---

[1] "Endgame" in Samuel Beckett, *The Complete Dramatic Works* (London: Faber, 1986), p. 101.

mind is ready for ridicule, for bathos, for mockery. "You thought *what* would happen if you left that door open?! You didn't *really* think that would happen, did you? How ridiculous! How *funny*!"

The worrier's habits aren't impossible to enjoy. There's that which is authentically amusing in our obsessions as well as our inability to keep conclusions from spinning out of control. Repetitions can be funny. So can the reasoning of anxiety, partly because it *is* reasoning, or at least has the appearance of it. The English novelist and journalist Jerome K. Jerome (1859–1927) made some fun out of "hypochondria" (in the modern health-related sense of the term) in the opening scene of his parody of imperial adventure, *Three Men in a Boat (To say Nothing of the Dog)* (1889), a comic novel still much read. J., the narrator, is absorbed with the failings of his own body. And he reveals, at the beginning of the story, just how easily diagnoses can get out of hand:

> I remember going to the British Museum one day to read up the treatment for some slight ailment of which I had a touch—hay fever, I fancy it was. I got down the book, and read all I came to read; and then, in an unthinking moment, I idly turned the leaves, and began to indolently study diseases, generally. I forget which was the first distemper I plunged into—some fearful, devastating scourge, I know—and, before I had glanced half down the list of "premonitory symptoms," it was borne in upon me that I had fairly got it.
>
> I sat for awhile, frozen with horror; and then, in the listlessness of despair, I again turned over the pages. I came to typhoid fever— read the symptoms—discovered that I had typhoid fever, must have had it for months without knowing it—wondered what else I had got; turned up St. Vitus's Dance—found, as I expected, that I had that too,—began to get interested in my case, and determined to sift it to the bottom, and so started alphabetically—read up ague,

and learnt that I was sickening for it, and that the acute stage would commence in about another fortnight. Bright's disease, I was relieved to find, I had only in a modified form, and, so far as that was concerned, I might live for years. Cholera I had, with severe complications; and diphtheria I seemed to have been born with. I plodded conscientiously through the twenty-six letters, and the only malady I could conclude I had not got was housemaid's knee.[2]

The joke's a risky one and on the borders of bad taste. Most of these diseases—cholera, diphtheria, typhoid—were terrible killers in the nineteenth century. Bright's Disease, a nineteenth-century term for a serious kidney complaint, is hardly the stuff of sparkling laughter either. But the amusement lies in the disjunction between the starting point in J.'s mind—has he a touch of hay fever?—and the dismal catalog he ends up with. Hay fever was first recorded in the 1820s and it was hardly a complaint of virile masculinity. The passage plays, in turn, with the nervous effeminacy that readily surrounds men who fret about illness. It codes J. and his friends as not quite red-blooded. Yet the comedy doesn't lie in the "unmanly" response but in a disjunction between the starting point and the end point. The amusingly disturbing element of the passage is that J.'s conclusions are apparently evidence-based. They're deductions from a reasoned consideration of the "facts" matched against the specific diagnoses found in the medical dictionary. And they're wildly off the mark.

Sorrow and sadness have a long tradition in English—and perhaps particularly in England—of sparking laughter that's not quite cruel or callous but which grows out of pain, in a durable relationship between two things that ought not to belong. Worry is merely an example of that unlikely but persisting companionship. Worry's

---

[2]Jerome K. Jerome, *Three Men in a Boat (To Say Nothing of the Dog)* (Bristol: Arrowsmith, 1889), pp. 2–3.

repetitive patterns can be like taglines or catchphrases. As if we are characters in a novel by Charles Dickens or the translator in Jonathan Safran Foer's brilliantly harrowing *Everything is Illuminated* (2002), worriers have to hand phrases and motifs that immediately identify us, even if only to ourselves. We have leitmotifs and mottos, and we're like comic characters on stage who say the same thing, who respond in the same way.

Sometimes the very seriousness of worry, its po-faced earnestness about itself and its own condition, is funny. Sometimes, for better or for worse, worries can only be met with a laugh. In the real world, often enough, there's little else to do. "You cannot be *that* serious!?" "You can't mean me to respond other than with a smile at such absurdity?" Laughing at the ridiculous is, in its way, the mark of human failure to change the bizarre conditions in which we live. But it's also a result of the fact that absurdity *is* funny. It's *so* ridiculous I can only laugh. Sisyphus, pushing his stone up a hill, is a tragic figure of the modern man. But he also makes us bleakly smile.

Laughing at, or in, worry helps reconcile us to it. And that's a faint pointer to another way of thinking about the business of fretting. If only we could take away the *pain* of worrying, the headaches of anxiety, the racing pulse, the sheer misery of apprehension, the sleeplessness, or just the plain heaviness of heart that accompanies the worrier into the ordinary world, then there are, it may be, some decent things to be said about worrying. Oddly, worrying might even do us some good. Thinking like a worrier has its potential compensation—apart from the actual worrying, that is.

I've claimed grandly that the worrier is in an advantageous position to see through some of the assumptions of intellectual liberalism and the problematic world created by Choice Theory. But there's more to say, more modestly. The evolutionary advantages of serious kinds of mental illness are widely discussed—even if they're not agreed.

One of the ways of making sense of mental illness is to say that it makes sense in itself. Serious mental problems, in this argument, are part of human life for a reason. Lacking God, often enough, the modern evolutionary scientist can only attribute such sense to God's replacement: the indifferent but still, it appears, helpful forces of evolutionary biology.

Charles Rycroft, a British psychoanalyst and psychotherapist, considered some of these evolutionary advantages in 1968 in an influential book called *Anxiety and Neurosis*. Rycroft thought anxiety was a kind of protection against more serious mental sickness. Anxiety was a natural prophylactic against the mind's psychological deterioration. Unlike the earlier writers on worry who sometimes feared that worry was the start of a dismal decline into grave mental sickness, Rycroft thought the opposite. He argued that the evolutionary function of low-level "anxiety" was that it protected the individual *against* becoming crazy. Anxiety, he proposed, "is a form of vigilance which occurs after one has encountered danger, problem or opportunity but before one has been aware of its exact nature and thus before one knows whether one is still on familiar territory."[3] That vigilance could be valuable and protective. It gives us the ability to guard ourselves against dangers both physical and mental.

I don't find it difficult to see logic in the claim that worry might be a way of identifying problems and potential solutions before they become worse or, even, unmanageable. In one respect, that's only a way of saying that what we worry about really does matter. It's a way of saying that worry helps us—albeit painfully—to deal with life's challenges by anticipating them. Worrying is a condition that encourages us to stay on top, to make the best preparations. Without pain, no doubt, we wouldn't take future problems so seriously and

---

[3]Charles Rycroft, *Anxiety and Neurosis* (Harmondsworth: Penguin, 1968), p. 16.

in turn we'd endanger ourselves. That's plainly true about practical matters. If I worry about catching an important train tomorrow morning, it means that I'm at the train station in good time with my prepurchased ticket and my reserved seat (and possibly even my mobile phone). In turn, I've a better chance of arriving at my destination having sat down all the way, relieved and on time. That's a form of vigilance against problems, if only at the most mundane level. Of course, it doesn't exactly help worriers very much to remind us that, actually, what we worry about *does* matter and that things will be worse if we cheerfully accept things as they come. But it's still helpful to be told that worry isn't unhappiness without issue, that there's some gain to it. Worry's motivating and in a strange way enabling. What do the authors of self-help books think about claims that there's purpose to worry, that even if worry brings suffering, it still helps keep us safe? Curing worry could be taking the safety-harness off.

There's a bolder argument about the evolutionary advantages not of worry but of depression. This suggests the "usefulness" of mental troubles on a larger scale but helps, perhaps, to reinforce the sense that mental pains of various kinds have a purpose. Paul Keedwell in *How Sadness Survived: The Evolutionary Basis of Depression* (2008) thinks that depression is a reminder, simply put, of what is important in human life (particularly, i.e. Western human life as he understands it). Dr Keedwell says that depression is a kind of conscience or monitor of values that can act as a brake on belief systems that have gone awry. Depression is a check on ways of living that don't correspond to what Keedwell thinks are fundamental, inherited human requirements. Depression occurs when archetypal needs, as he sees it, aren't met. Such needs include safe homes or places to live; food and drink; the care of parents early in life; a working partnership in later life; and membership of a social group that also gives an individual a role and status. Immediately, the word "need" strikes a warning bell since ideological assumptions and oppressions can easily be smuggled into general statements from one human being about what every other human being "needs." We know that from parental views: "what Edmund needs is to get a job and settle down with a nice girl." Well, maybe—but maybe not. There's something heavy-handed, potentially oppressive, about this description of what we all need. Nevertheless, Keedwell's framework of ancestral and permanent desires in human life leads him to the thought-provoking observation that depression's a reminder that we've gone off-course. We've become absorbed by things that aren't fundamental and given ourselves the wrong priorities.

One of Dr Keedwell's examples is Marco. As for many a therapist, Keedwell's life narratives of patients or clients are essential in his theory of mental health: diagnosis and cure are derived from a therapist's capacity to interpret a human story. Those stories, in turn, have to be retold in a book and so must be made "story-shaped." The life stories must reveal patterns and be "readable"; they must comprise a sequence of cause-and-effect and have an exemplary logic. There's little room for the accidental or the incoherent: there's no room for the simply unknown, the baffling, the unaccounted-for, the random. Such is the power and influence of narrative—narrative's very necessity—in understanding mental health as any reader of Sigmund Freud's detectivelike versions of psychologies knows.

Marco used to live a whirlwind life in a city job designing sets for fashion shows and department stores. He lived at a fast pace but with deep fears of being rejected; with a serious problem of self-esteem; a stressful profession; and a fearsome cocaine habit. Marco slowly became depressed. And, in being depressed, he was forced to evaluate what his life was like; what he was living for; what his "life goals" were. He had to think how far adrift his priorities were from the archetypal needs that Dr Keedwell believes we inherit from our forefathers. Marco gave up his old life. He now lives on a yacht.

Marco's view is coherent with Dr Keedwell's conclusions and Marco
comes to be Keedwell's spokesman. Marco believes, apparently, that
everyone should experience depression because it reveals who you
are. Through depression primary needs are made real and visible,
and in the extremes of this suffering what is important stands out
like a firework display.[4] Dr Keedwell's view of what are, as I say,
"fundamental needs" is problematic. They depend, apart from
anything else, on some speculation on what primitive human life was
like ("Psychologically, we are still living in the caves," he says[5]) though
his claims are, naturally, without any evidence. Some might think his
list of "archetypal needs" not primitive but bourgeois, or, at the very
least, ideologically weighted and historically conditioned by his own
assumptions, class, gender, nationality, and historical environment.
St Evagrius, for a start, wouldn't recognize them. Dr Keedwell has the
same problem as every writer who uses "case histories" (including
me, of course). How far is Marco *real*? How far is this case history
shaped to fit an argument? I don't say this with anything other than
sympathy for Dr Keedwell because my own "case histories" are partly
disguised and no doubt I am, at some level, shaping the evidence
to fit my preconceived theories. There's the belief-then-reasoning
problem again.

But the broad claim that there's an evolutionary advantage to
"sadness" and that is why it has survived is engaging, all the same.
Depression here, in the most general sense, is an indication and
even an education in what we're doing wrong; it's evidence that we've
made some miscalculation in our values, some misjudgment in our
behavior and some mistake in what we think's right. Such a theory

---

[4]See Paul Keedwell, *How Sadness Survived: The Evolutionary Basis of Depression* (Oxford:
Radcliffe, 2008), p. 31.
[5]Ibid., p. 4.

places us back with the self-help therapists who, showing that we have the power to heal ourselves, also allow us to infer that our suffering is, to some degree, our own responsibility and in our own power to change. I've some anxiety about how easily such an argument can become ideological or political. But is it, I ask myself, still useful to think of *worry* as the result, in any way, of an error I have made, a mistake, a false move? Is it useful to think of the worrier's troubles, far down on the scale of pain from depression, as a result of a mental or emotional slipup?

Worry arises, in the most general of terms, from the confluence of historical, theological, and economic circumstances with personal traits and histories. Of the personal qualities that create worry, an inner sense of security and robustness in dealing with the world must be the best defense against fretfulness. One of the most common side effects or manifestations of insecurity is, undoubtedly, a high level of self-criticism or self-dissatisfaction. The early self-help books, and their descendents, are ready to reach for the language of rebuke, of reprobation. But no-one blames the worrier quite so much as the worrier blames him or herself. We worriers have often effortlessly internalized the "It's Your Responsibility" argument and distorted it in the process. We've swallowed the self-help books' aims to empower us and turned them into an ugly conclusion. We think not only that we're to blame for feeling unhappy but also that we're to blame if others are unhappy because of our mistakes; our lack of vigilance; our failure to worry enough; our failure to act adequately on the basis of our worries. The language of reprobation, of retribution, has infected us so that we're haunted by a dread that we're responsible if things go amiss for those affected by our ill-managed actions. We're bothered that we'll "spoil" things, that things will be *our fault*.

Leaving the back door open might be bad enough if I lived in this house on my own. But part of the source of my worry—sitting at work, far away from being able to check—is that those who live with me will be affected by my carelessness in leaving the door unlocked. Their lives will be upset by burglars, their routines troubled, their possessions taken, their sense of security spoilt. This feeling of mine shouldn't be mistaken for altruism or responsibility. It is, at its core, selfish. The trouble that most concerns me is perhaps not spoiling another's happiness but giving them cause to rebuke me. How much of my worry isn't an act of vigilance against problems that I'd be wise to avoid—a serious disease, a domestic accident, a stolen car—but an act of vigilance on behalf of my own hyperconscious self, fearful of criticism, fearful of having to say sorry?

With such an analysis, I can see a case for understanding worry—in part—as a product of a personal mistake. And understanding that mistake makes the worrier think about vanity. The mistake of the worriers, here, is to think too highly of ourselves. The mistake is to think that we should *not* make mistakes; the mistake is to think that we are too good to err and certainly too good to admit errors or apologize for them. We may fear apologizing because, we tell ourselves, we're already so self-critical that admitting to another person that we've made a mistake takes us just too low in our own self-esteem. We're berated enough from inside! But in truth we may fear apologizing because we're too proud to admit that we can be wrong; too egotistical and defensive to allow ourselves to err in our own or in another's eyes. This proud "fear" of error may arise, too, from the fact that we think ourselves "in charge" of the happiness of others, that we believe our actions are the most significant influence on their well-being. "If I make a mistake, then their day is ruined . . ." But this, too, may be another mask for pride; another visor for vanity. I have to check with myself as frequently as I can, when worrying about someone else, whether my worry comes from a lurking sense that I'm the important person, the person who can make or mar the happiness of another.

Perhaps the worrier might relax, then, by being a bit more—humble. It's not a popular word. It's almost been wholly banished from daily discourse not least because Charles Dickens's Uriah Heep in *David Copperfield* (1849–50) has persuaded us that 'umility is always 'ypocritical and that it's a cover for self-interest. Humility can easily feel like the cloak under which oppressors smuggle in obedience, unquestioning acceptance. But it's of use to me. If worry, in a small part, is the product of the mistake I've been describing earlier then the solution—at least, a partial way of relieving the pain—is to moderate expectation; to be kinder to myself; to accept that I fail; to be ready to apologize; to be ready to take criticism.

Defensiveness may feel as if it is rooted in a frail and unconfident self. Yet it may rather be rooted in something like conceit. It's not often that one might take Lady Macbeth as a model for a counselor. But, for all her blood-soaked cruelty, there's something, just for a moment, which might interest a worrier. Oddly enough, Lady Macbeth seems initially more willing to accept the possibility of failure in her ghastly plans to make Macbeth King of Scotland than her husband. If Shakespeare has a figure anywhere close to a worrier, it is Macbeth in Act 1 (and Hamlet, of course). Contemplating the treacherous murder of King Duncan at the beginning of the play, Macbeth attends to his wife's hearty criticism of him. But "If we should fail?" he finally inquires, to which, rather surprisingly, Lady Macbeth crisply replies, "We fail!" (1:7:59). Their purpose is obviously vile. That is not my point and neither is the long speech that Lady Macbeth then delivers, assuring her husband that failure will only come if he does not screw his courage to the sticking place. What's of interest is the acceptance, for the briefest moment, that failure may, simply, happen. It is, as Lady Macbeth appears to recognize in some part of her feral heart, a strangely enabling answer to fearfulness, to a worry about the future, to the question of "*what if . . .?*"

We worriers shouldn't assume that we are too good for failure, or too proud to deal with objections, or too grand to take responsibility for something that went wrong, or so grand that if anything goes wrong it *must* be our responsibility. Worry may be a form of barometer that might indicate to us, if we can read it correctly, that we could adjust our assumptions about our significance and relieve ourselves of the negative effects of wounded self-importance or all-too precarious pride.

It's amazing how quickly thinking about worry can turn me into a preacher. And, of course, I am, in a way, back to the troublesome and baffling matter of adjusting beliefs about myself, adjusting my inner sense of who I am by arguing for different ones. I have, it seems, stumbled inadvertently back onto my old problem with worry. I don't like the assumption of the self-help books that the way out of worry is to change my underlying beliefs about myself. I don't like their assumption about what those beliefs should be. Yet at the same time, it strikes me that thinking carefully about my own worry *can* expose underlying convictions, underlying ideas about who I am and how I'm perceived. Because I can see those beliefs clearly, I can indeed challenge and try to change them. I can recognize, for myself, that they are negatives that do me damage, that they cause me unnecessary and, so it seems, avoidable pain. The secret to this tangle, the key to this apparent contradiction, can only lie in the strength that *self*-discovery possesses. It must depend on the difference between identifying problems for myself as distinct from a self-help book or an analyst or a friend doing it for me. The secret appears to be in doing the thinking for myself. The secret lies, bizarrely enough, in the very condition of independent reasoning that helped bring worry into the world in the first place. Worry can suggest valuable knowledge about inner beliefs. But for that knowledge to be helpful, I think you have to have grasped it on your own.

Thinking: it's the activity from which worry is born. And it's also that on which all reasonable, rational life depends. There are other, more pragmatic things, to be said about the blessings of worry, far from any great "fundamental" needs of human beings. There are things to be said that concern the ordinary world that we daily live in. The business of asking questions, the insistent inquiries that worry breeds, can be valuable. Checking, considering things in detail, thinking about matters from different perspectives, and reconsidering, are natural inclinations of the worrier. Such questioning is the dye that our worriers' hands are subdued in. You can't often catch a worrier out (though being caught out, being shown another way of thinking about a risk that had not occurred to us, is something about which we worriers live in sweaty anticipation). Worriers enumerate: we list more than we evaluate; we collect impressions of implications more than we judge their likelihood. We run through options, assimilating and listening for the give-away sounds of ideas we haven't attended to. We're always alert to the snuffling in the undergrowth of bristly problems we've not already imagined. We're analysts of difficulties and dilemmas who are sometimes genuinely good at analyzing even if we take little pleasure in our gifts and frequently fail to adjudicate on the most likely outcomes. It's hard to get a worrier to make a decision or commit to a particular direction. But if you want an assessment of the possible consequences of decisions, then, well, you could do worse than to ask me.

We're not natural politicians because we don't easily make those decisions. We're instinctively not happy with action that does not take every view into account and, as a consequence, we are occasionally tempted by the opposite: of ruthless, careless, decision-making, just to prove that we can do it. We usually regret those moments. But we're good, or *could* be good, in the right circumstances, at describing to someone else what the possibilities are. A worrier has usually done his or her preparation, however nervously. We are, in one respect, a little like Mycroft Holmes, gifted with stronger analytical powers than Sherlock Holmes, his brother. Sherlock, in Arthur Conan Doyle's detective stories, is the decisive man, the man of action: the one who actually lies on the ground looking through his magnifying glass for clues; the one who lays traps for criminals in empty houses; who pursues enemies to the edge of waterfalls. Mycroft doesn't move from his limited daily round to and from his club. Often he doesn't move from his chair. But he does think.

A worrier might make, typically, a good and a bad lawyer all in one. Worriers, certainly, make better advisers than doers, of any sort. A worrier can see fresh angles, loopholes, ways in or ways out, which others often haven't noticed. We're adept at perceiving new interpretations of phrases and so, in the modern workplace, at advising others about carefully protected and well-defended positions; about contracts that cover many eventualities; about documents that don't leave holes through which money or time or reputation will leak. The worrier-advisor shouldn't have to make decisions—we must leave that to someone else—but we're deft at setting out the terms on which decisions could be made.

Portia in Shakespeare's *The Merchant of Venice* has obviously been thinking hard about the loopholes in the bond that Shylock, the moneylender, has extracted from Antonio, the merchant of the title. She suggests what would happen if a worrier and a lawyer were, I fondly imagine, trapped inside the same person. Shylock's bond requires a pound of Antonio's flesh if he defaults on a loan. When he *does* default, Shylock is determined to uphold the letter of the law. He is unmoved by Portia (disguised as the lawyer Balthazar) and her courtroom plea for mercy. So Portia must quibble. She must look for other implications and other byways that reason could follow. She bids Antonio prepare to die, as she encourages Shylock to be fussy about what exactly is and what is not in the original contract. Then she makes her move. "Tarry a little," Portia says with modest words that turn the direction of the whole play, just as the flesh is about to be sliced:

> There is something else.
> This bond doth give thee here no jot of blood.
> The words expressly are "a pound of flesh."
> Take then thy bond. Take thou thy pound of flesh.
> But in cutting it, if thou doest shed
> One drop of Christian blood, thy lands and goods
> Are by the law of Venice confiscate
> Unto the state of Venice.

(4:1:302–9)

Shylock can't say that the exact details of the contract are not important because he has already been explicit on this point. In turn, Portia wins the case by revealing that there is something they all have not thought about before. "There is something else," she says. Yes indeed. And it saves Antonio's life.

That ability to see another angle, as far as Antonio is concerned, makes a virtuous lawyer. But Portia's quibble is disturbing despite the fact that she prevents a man from dying. For here is thought that manages to outwit the obvious original intentions of a document, the obvious intentions of plain words. This is thinking that goes against the grain, which applies its own nifty counter-logic to sabotage unambiguous sense. Portia makes documents unstable, threatens to undo the conventions by which we communicate with each other (as she threatens to undo the conventions by which the law itself tries to work). There's something that the worrier can recognize in this ability to pull out an alternative possibility from what seemed clear enough, simple enough. As far as the law is concerned, another lawyer as good as Portia could, if statements are *this* susceptible to "misreading," presumably come up with *another* alternative reading in an effort to have that debt paid. This kind of thinking would end in confusion, in the failure to resolve anything. In Shakespeare's play, the result would be a drama that could not end except in "There is something else." The indecisiveness of the worrier's way of thinking is readable as a ghostly presence in this scene of decision, of clever thinking, of taking mental action. The doubleness of worry as advantage and as peril is here to discern. Here's a reminder not to forget the blessings of the worrier's scrutinizing habits of mind, and not to forget, in the unwritten scenes of *The Merchant of Venice*, the mess in which those habits can, potentially, result.

I'll stay, for a while longer, with these (qualified) advantages. There's a quality of thoroughness in the worrier's preparations. He or she has the comprehensiveness of cover that anxiety can peculiarly encourage. People who aren't worriers sometimes have to work hard to reflect on implications in ways that come naturally, like leaves on a tree, to the worrier. As an attribute for human relations, such an ability to consider different possibilities is not without its uses. It's a necessity for peacemakers; for working with collegial, collaborative, and sensitive attention to others; for being part of a diverse group that must function together. Although we can be vain, we're also dreadfully keen to please. The ability to see other viewpoints is essential for those who hope to solve problems through negotiation rather than command; through discussion rather than dictation; through committees rather than from the director's chair. That ability is the necessary attribute for a human being who notices that others are different and hopes at least to try to take that difference into account.

I know, of course, that such ways of thinking and behaving don't always result in consensus or agreement or peace. I know that worriers are, as I've said, visited by the thin specter of John Stuart Mill and the failure of the liberal dream, the failure in practice of efforts to take everything on board, the failure to address and reply to all viewpoints in the belief that they'll be brought together in agreement. But I'm allowing myself to talk for a moment optimistically and to look for something, however cautiously, to admire. I know what the problems are. But I don't want wholly to forget that worriers have traits on which, despite evidence otherwise, we could still build some hope.

Worriers are reasonably good on their own. We don't need to be entertained. Classical wisdom suggests that one of the hardest things human beings can do is to sit in a room on their own. T. S. Eliot's speaker in "Ash Wednesday" longed to be taught "to sit still."[6] But the worrier's mind is always full of dialogue, of analysis, of reflection, so that sitting still, lingering on one's own, doesn't create too much of a vacancy. We certainly don't need anyone to teach us how to do it. We worriers live mostly in our own minds anyway. It hardly matters if there are others around. There's plenty going on inside to keep us occupied.

Worriers are often in careers that require thought and provide, at least in theory, time for thinking. We make the most of ideas. We are philosophers-in-ordinary. We're the quiet, local, modern, and entirely unremarkable inheritors of the School of Athens. We're perhaps the monks of the old days in new clothes, too; the theologians and the scholars, made freshly commonplace, newly familiar on the streets and in the offices. Even if we can hardly claim our inner thoughts to be intellectual ones, we live the life of the mind all the same. And because we're particularly good at thinking about words, and hidden meanings, worriers may be well-situated to make the most of what they read: history, politics, novels, poetry. Certainly, worriers may be particularly suited as readers of literature, strictly defined: of

---

[6]Eliot, *Collected Poems*, p. 96.

imaginative works of word art—plays, poems, fiction. There were more users of the university's counseling service from students of English literature than from any other department in my former university. I am sure that's not exceptional.

Worriers are good at analyzing states of mind, responses, nuances, the fine shades of feeling. No wonder we need the counseling service. And the very business of literary criticism, in some of its forms, might even be thought a *practice* of worry. We worry away at meanings and get into the habit of thinking that more is being said than first appears; that there are hidden implications we must track down. When the young undergraduate student William Empson (1906–84) set out his somewhat mathematically minded views on the multiple meanings of words in literature in *Seven Types of Ambiguity* (1930), he created a worry-reader's text book. Empson examined the capacity of words to create meanings that affirmed, extended, resisted, or flatly contradicted other meanings. He was interested in the different accounts each word or sentence could give of itself, in how many different ways a word or sentence could suggest different simultaneous meanings, even meanings that resulted in radical contradiction (that is the seventh type of ambiguity). Empson, something like a magnified version of Portia reading the law, has been influential in the formal study of English literature in the United Kingdom and the United States. Many of his assumptions about how we can read poetry, in particular, remain. Worriers, worrying *at* things and ready to pick out the hidden implications of words, might know better than many what William Empson was talking about.

The worrier knows that pain is part of the substance of life. The largest use of the worrier's way of looking at things may simply be to take worrying as a counter to the bland cheeriness that's crept into assumptions of what our life is now supposed to be. The worrier has a better grasp on the reality of life's mixture, its compounds of pleasure and of sorrow, than the recommended, approved pleasures that define how we are meant to be today. Eric G. Wilson's *Against Happiness: In Praise of Melancholy* (2008) is a witty argument against the superficial contentment of the modern-day commercial culture of the United States as contrasted with what he thinks a darker, more melancholy Europe. But superficial pleasures are far from unfamiliar to Europeans. We know the happiness promised by the advertisements, the "Have a nice day" of the checkout clerks, the cheerful image of a deity that wants us all to be worshippers reassured of our own capacity for pleasure. Wilson could discover new depths to European shallowness. But his point is that important human achievements—in art and in the history of ideas—come primarily from sorrow. The best arts arise from a realization of the troubles and unresolvable dilemmas of being alive. *Sunt lacrimae rerum* (*Aeneid*, i.462): "Tears in the nature of things."[7] The superficial pleasures of the modern West are a betrayal, Wilson thinks, of how things really are. Such pleasures are a form of oppression that drives us crazy with an expectation that we should all be blandly happy. And pale, inch-deep happiness is no basis for lasting cultural or artistic achievement.

Happiness can do more damage. A blithe confidence that all will work out may be exactly the reason of why it won't. Happiness can be a distraction; a smokescreen that hides a deep failure to look at problems as they really are: problems of politics and economics, of the security of the globe itself. Sometimes a mere faith in the future is a lazy way of avoiding problems that must be tackled. Roger Scruton's *The Uses of Pessimism and the Danger of False Hope* (2010) is a bracing argument about the damage done to Western cultures by an unintelligent, uncritical, hope. Scruton, in favor of limiting optimism,

---

[7]Virgil, *The Aeneid*, p. 20.

wants a dose of suspicion and fretfulness to regulate human folly in planning for the future. Barbara Ehrenreich is bleaker as she considers in greater political detail the same cheerfulness that dismays Wilson. Her *Smile or Die: How Positive Thinking Fooled America & the World* (2009) is a tonic for the complainer, a support for the moaner and the cynic. Her book makes even us furtive, almost invisible, worriers feel important. *Smile or Die* champions the negative thought that's urgently needed, Ehrenreich proposes, to prevent a false "positive thinking" from contributing, in foreign policy, health care, environmental policy, economics, and elsewhere, to disaster. More displeasure, more unhappiness, more discontent, more *worry*: these things have a political use and they are, paradoxically, what will help make an insecure future more secure.

Worriers are hardly the best prophets of the world's future. But it turns out that we may be something of what's needed. Our reluctance to be optimistic is the state of mind that's missing from a pernicious pursuit of smiles. Our inbuilt suspicion of the simplistic discourses of happiness, our natural disinclination to be fooled by uninformed, deliberate certainties of positive thinking (or at least, fooled for very long), are conditions to which, it may be, we should all aspire. Our state of mind is one from which our politicians could learn. We worriers are not naturally at home with joyful prognostications. Our *métier* is not the optimists' and our natural habitat is far from those who would tell us to stop frowning and simply "have a nice day." We're haunted by the tremulous uncertainties of *"what if . . .?"* Bothered about the future, we worriers might well be on the side of more realistic prospects; a future where problems have been recognized rather than hidden; acknowledged rather than smuggled away behind a Disney-land grin.

It's an encouraging thought, paradoxically, that mental pain might be a good thing. But that doesn't really stop me wanting to be free from worries. I might be useful. Yet I still have fugitive longings for the happiness that I can best define in the negative: a contentment that's worry-free. Worries can be incorrigible and ineradicable. They can be more or less impossible to remove, spreading like a permanent dye in the mind. Worries linger under the surface of daily life, distracting me from the conversation. Worries flood into silences with their sludgy presence and they can't easily be cleaned out. Often enough, however much we try to look for the advantages of worry, the best for which we can often hope is not for peace but temporary peace: not the lifting of worries but a moment's forgetfulness; a brief respite, thinking of something else. Worry's peculiarly attended by a desire for that which is temporary because it's only the temporary that's achievable. Glimpses define worry's usual ambitions for tranquility. Because there are no durable solutions, there can only be moments that worriers enjoy. We are, inevitably, attracted to the short term; to that which we shouldn't analyze for long.

We're in a perpetual courtship with the fleeting. Few describe that better than W. H. Auden, the poet who thought hard about the nature of the newly named modern disease. His "A Summer Night" recalls a time when Auden worked as a school teacher in a small independent school. Some summer nights were so warm that the resident staff brought their mattresses to the school lawns and slept outside. These were times of exceptional pleasure, Auden recalled—memorable many years afterward. They were evenings when

> Fear gave his watch no look;
> The lion griefs loped from the shade
> And on our knees their muzzles laid,
> And Death put down his book.[8]

---

[8]Auden, *Collected Poems*, p. 117.

That's an elegantly conceived vision of a worry-free moment. There's no fear, no sorrow, and even the greatest of troubles, a fear of death, is for a moment lifted, forgotten. Of course, the reader knows that this isn't going to last. Death hasn't gone away and lions don't remain quiet for long. But for the time being, what had troubled before has, for a moment, become a companion. The griefs are tame, for now.

Where in human experience, for the worrier, *are* the times without worry? Where can the worry-less best be experienced? Samuel Johnson (1709–84), the eighteenth-century lexicographer, would, I reckon, have been a worrier had he lived in the twentieth century. As far as his dogged Scottish biographer, James Boswell (1740–95), was concerned, it was definitely work that kept off his demons. "[Johnson] is now to be considered as 'tugging at his oar,'" Boswell said, describing the end of 1747, "as engaged in a steady continued course of occupation, sufficient to employ all his time for some years." This was, he went on, "the best preventive of that constitutional melancholy which was ever lurking about him, ready to trouble his quiet."[9] Work is an antidote for "melancholy" as it is sometimes for worry. But distracting labor is not the only thing. For the surest place where worry cannot easily be is in the memory. We can recall that we were worried in the past but we can't easily revive or relive the worry itself. We can remember the experience but not exactly recuperate it.

The dominant question of worry is a question about the future— "*what if . . .?*"—and, mercifully, that can't be asked very sensibly about the past. The future is already known, the outcome of "*what if . . .?*" isn't in doubt. The results of decisions have occurred; the people involved have discovered what the consequences were, for better or for worse. We worriers might not like the consequences or we might be used to them. But there's no need to worry about the decisions themselves

---

[9]*Boswell's Life of Johnson*, ed. G. B. Hill, 6 vols (New York: Bigelow, Brown, n.d.), i.209.

because they have been made. Worry about the future hardly has a home in the past. The historical anxieties can be studied—and we can regret decisions that we or others made, believing them to have been wrong. We can even try to undo the consequences. A lot of human and institutional problems are, I am slowly understanding, heritage ones: problems that haven't been solved or even acknowledged from the past. But we can't feel *worried* about the consequences of an event that we already know has taken place. We can't worry about the "*what if . . .?*" question if the "if" has already been made irrelevant. The nineteenth-century British Prime Minister Robert Peel (1788–1850) might have been perturbed about whether to repeal of the Corn Laws or not. But we can't worry for him now even if, in some ways, we're still living with the consequences of that tough step against protectionism. The Irish builders of *RMS Titanic* might well have fretted about the security of the ship's design, despite all the hype. They might have wondered if that rudder was really large enough, those sea doors really adequate, those lifeboats numerous enough. But we can't *worry* with them all over again even if we know they worried in the first place.

This is all the more the case with personal histories. Worriers may be often better at enjoying things after they've happened. Happiness belongs, in our conception, most securely in the past because it *is* secure there. Worriers are pleased with pleasures taken and it's anticipation of pleasures that's the troublesome matter. We take more pleasure in holidays when they are concluded and can be safely enjoyed in memories that expunge worry: worry about unexpected travel costs; worry about the train not arriving on time; the hotel being noisy or hot or overpriced; the hire car being stolen or damaged; the food being expensive and poor; the mosquito bites; worry about our house being safe while we are away; the holiday itself being less enjoyable than last year's; the speed with which the holiday will be over and we have to go back to work. The pain of such troubles is, more or less, erased by memory. Or at least those worries cease to worry us because we know that everything was all right, we had a good time, and the house was fine. Now it's over, I can sit back and enjoy my holiday.

Do worriers tend to visit the same places, go to the same restaurants, and take the same trips? Are we naturally inclined to do things they have already done because there are fewer worries? Is there something habitually *memorial* about the worrier's journeys? That's to say, do we make journeys that are defined by memory and in them pay implicit tribute to a past that we're trying to maintain because it's more sure than the unexpected and the new? Doing the same thing over again is, I guess, a trademark of the worrier: a technique of worry management that finds in adventure something best avoided. This retrospective fascination, the tug of the worry-less in history, makes me especially interested in photographs. Personal photographs have a peculiar attraction. Certainly, photography has a close association with the memorial, with nostalgia, even with mourning. And it's a good medium for persuading us that we "own" the past or that we *belong* to places and times now gone. Susan Sontag sensibly says that "photographs give people and imaginary possession of a past that is unreal [and] also help people to take possession of space in which they are insecure."[10] Photographs of locations new to us, perhaps those visited while on holiday, provide a way of imaginatively making us "at home" somewhere that'd been new and potentially threatening, potentially worrying. Photography undertakes the harmonizing or calming work of adhesion, persuading us, when we look back, that we were safe somewhere where we weren't.

Photographs of a worrier's past may bring a set of painful reflections: "oh, didn't I look young then!" But they're also gently tranquilizing because we can look at them without wondering what happened next.

---

[10]Susan Sontag, *On Photography* (London: Penguin, 1979), p. 9.

Sontag famously remarks that all photographs are "*memento mori*," reminders of death. "To take a photograph," she says, is to "participate in another person's (or thing's) mortality, vulnerability, mutability."[11] But, for a worrier, there is something more life-enhancing than that. Photographs may be touched with sorrow but they're also little pools what relieve anxiety. They offer a glimpse of a time where worry can't be relived even if we worry about the *passage* of time since the photo was taken. Photographs are attractive, too, because they permit worriers to fantasize meanings visually, to imagine what was going on in the minds and feelings of others in the past. To consider a picture of smiling people round a restaurant table, or in front of some sun-soaked landscape, allows me to fantasize an idea of contentment through an image. That pleasure may not have been there. There may have been many other things than good cheer behind those smiling faces. But, hoping for the best, for a sign that there *are* other ways of living than with worry, the worrier can for a moment pretend.

I think worriers imagine pleasures more easily with visual images than with anything else. Looking at the words of the past—old letters, old emails, diaries, postcards—can bring real old troubles back with more bite. Such things involve our minds too much because they involve words. Images have a better chance of being reassuring because they are riper for fantasy, more ready for glossing over.

People can be objects of fantasy too. Maybe there's something of the stalker, the voyeur, the lingerer about the worrier. If we can sit alone, worrying, occupied by the drama of our own minds, we are also the familiar of others, an attendant on the lives of men and women who seem to be handling things better. We're great, and often injudicious, admirers. Worriers may spend time looking at art or listening to music, trying to get away from the noise in their heads. But there's

---

[11]Ibid., p. 15.

also a lot hanging around to do. If photographs or representations of the apparently untroubled, or the beyond-troubling, have a quiet consolation or at least enable a fantasy of it, the unknown lives of real people offer more vital possibilities. Actual human beings bring more living reassurance just by being imagined. The worrier is a great secret fantasist. He or she is keen to cherish others when they appear to be unlike themselves. If worriers find it hard to shift their belief about themselves, they don't find it so difficult to fabricate something to believe about others.

The worrier may find pleasure in being among those who seem to be, or are, at ease. We find pleasure attending to those who are, or appear to be, in confident possession of themselves. Unchecked admiration, a sentimental attachment to those we hardly know, persistently tempts the worrier in his or her hope to find alternative models of how to be. Rather than choose to be different, we can at least endeavor to enjoy the not-us of others' lives. This can momentarily relieve, or distract, the troubles of being who we are. Worriers gain a kind of bloodless but still vampiric strength from the surety of others about whom they have no certain knowledge, even from those whom they'll never know and never see again. Friends won't do because we know them. Parents and partners will do even less. We need a largely blank page on which to write our meanings. We need only a few hints from that nearly unknown other: of confidence or contentment, of strength or purpose. And that's enough. We need the smallest amount of knowledge about those who are only, and temporarily, on the outermost margin of our understanding. We need the wonderful and affirmative possibilities of what's almost certainly not true.

Beaches and department stores, sports grounds and choirs, pubs and museums, hotels and gardens: they're all decent enough, familiar enough places where the worrier may take not his or her own pleasure but the pleasure of others. Social networking sites, with all their potential as virtual spaces for the theatrical performance of private lives, offer another location for the drawing of strength from probable fictions. Those distant figures, reached only through cyberspace, are available as antidotes for the worriers' condition. It's the chance, the possibility, the hint, which matters. The Irish studies academic Luke Gibbons thinks that social networking sites diminish intimacy.[12] But intimacy is not all we want. The very distance such sites create between human beings is liberating. That distance allows us to admire those we hardly know. Imagining the inner life of other people, conceiving of them as possessing strengths that are not the worrier's, is a worrier's luxury. Looking beyond ourselves can help us. The worrier might be a little jealous of the unworrying dead. But he or she can draw furtive moments of contentment from fantasies of security and happiness woven around the living too.

Worry can hardly live in memory. And it can live even less in that which we can't remember at all, among that which is not part of us any way. I wonder how many visitors to ancient monuments, to museums and medieval churches, to ancestral houses and archaeological digs, are secretly aware of places where they can imagine, however dimly, the worry-less, the worry-free. We find some consolation in thinking of times and places where, if worry was, it wasn't ours. Part of the magic and enchantment of such places is remoteness from our own minds and histories. As visitors, we might be enjoying, unconsciously, a point in time where the worries of the past are far distanced. "*What if . . .?*" doesn't matter anymore among the histories of other men and women. If I can't stop worrying, I can at least take warmth from visiting that which doesn't bother any longer. Do some worriers

[12]Article in the *Irish Examiner*, July 24, 2010: available at http://www.examiner.ie/ireland/internet-damages-intimate-relationships-says-academic-126097.html, accessed August 11, 2010.

haunt graveyards, too, or battlefields, or wrecks, or even old sites of gallows (our house is actually on such a site)? Are we capable of being odd kinds of macabre tourists seeking not the life of the dead but their very deadness? A worrier may be worrying about death, what Clive Lilwall in *How to Stop Your 67 Worse Worries* (2004), calls the "lifelong worry."[13] But at least, in the necropolis, we are among those who are not.

The past *can* be a worry, of course. Looking at its remains is one thing. But wondering about how our own personal past could have been different is another. Despite what I've said, there are occasions when the really committed worrier can reinscribe "*what if . . .?*" back into history and fret that things could have turned out differently. "*If only. . . .*" That's the trouble the American poet Robert Frost (1874–1963) called "The Road not Taken." Irritated at being squeezed out of memory in contemplations of the completion of the past, its "over-and-done-with-deciding," worry can make a peevish reentry in thoughts about how life could have been different if only other decisions had been made. Worriers may be peculiarly prey to the temptation of imagining a better life *if only* something had been decided differently for them or by them: "if only I had gone to that other school; if only we hadn't moved house; if only my Spanish teacher had been more inspiring . . ." Such retrospections are tempting, to different degrees, because they allow worriers to fantasize another way of being without having to do much about it. Here's the rather vain comfort of knowing that my life has turned out in ways for which I'm not responsible and can't do anything to change now. There's an odd tranquility in wondering about what could have been different when it's too late to change.

---

[13]See Clive Lilwall, *How to Stop Your 67 Worse Worries* (Bloomington: Authorhouse, 2004), pp. 1–27.

Photographs allow us to invent moments seemingly free from worry. Certainly, we can make a heartening imaginative investment in them as such, bargaining with images for a glossy glimpse of something still. And beyond these little local instances of Kodak-powered peace, there's pleasure for a worrier in the tranquil altogether. Worry may be in the brain but many things that come in through the eyes can help. Giovanni Bellini's pictures offer scenes of calm acceptance, inner and outer serenity. I've sat for ages in front of Bellini's golden altarpiece in the sacristy of the church of the Frari in Venice. It's one of my favorite pictures. Bellini painted the altarpiece for exactly the spot where it remains: the altarpiece is in the exact location it was intended for, even as Bellini has depicted men and women who, confidently, know that what's planned for them. Cimabue, Giotto, Fra' Angelico are, likewise, painters of certainty and security—artists from the Age of Faith.

Objects or representations that are free from tempest, pain, or suffering can speak, for a moment, to the worrier. There's grace in art, it may be: a secret ministry. Of course, the capacity of art to touch the embarrassing troubles of the inner life is not easy to speak about. We lack a vocabulary for this intimate and highly subjective form of meaning. But the worrier knows it particularly. I'm talking of glimpses, still, and there's hardly enough in those snatched apprehensions to build much of a theory of aesthetics on. But the sensations of peace, of the lion griefs loping from the shade, are as real as they are welcome.

The Romanian-born Constantin Brâncuşi's Modernist sculptures include his *Bird in Space*, an abstract representation of motion that is absolutely static. There are various versions, several on display in his workshops in the center of Paris; the Peggy Guggenheim has one in Venice. Andrew Graham-Dixon described *Bird in Space* as "a curve of aspiring bronze as simple and piercing as a samurai swordblade, dissolves into a multiplicity of different graceful trajectories as the

viewer circles it, each like a different flight through space."[14] Graceful
is right—and "grace," a gift of art, is worth thinking about. But the
idea of a sword-blade doesn't seem correct to me. The curving form
is not violent, not mixed up with human confrontation or death
or ritual. The essence of this delicate but vibrantly strong object is
balance. Here's movement that's in repose: every new angle reveals
the refined curve of a highly polished shape, at rest. *Bird in Space*
proposes, to my mind at any rate, a glimpse of a world without
fretfulness. The worry-free is shaped into polished bronze, a form
of smoothness that, in its promise, relieves the viewer of troubles
for a moment. Modernism might coincide with modern culture's
discovery and exploitation of worry's name. But Brâncuşi's envisaged
Modernist forms that lift our view, for a moment, above the Disease
of the Age.

Pictures and objects, imaginatively entered, may free the viewer
for a moment or two from the pressure of worry, from its warty,
snuffling presence. So can sound. Of course, what we hear can be a
peculiar prompt for worry. Worry may be in the brain but sounds
can help put it there. The distant car alarm, the high-pitched whine
of electricity, the spluttering of a petrol engine, the unexpected noise
from downstairs in the middle of the night, the odd rumbling of an
airplane engine mid-flight are, none of them, conducive to ease. But
sound needn't be like this. Bird song—the blackbird singing in the
middle of a city early in the morning, a skylark invisibly singing above
a ploughed field—are charming voices from, it seems, another realm.
The very otherness of the bird or animal world is a reminder how
different things can be. Percy Bysshe Shelley (1792–1822), the English
Romantic poet, knew that. Listening to the skylark, he thought of how

---

[14]http://www.andrewgrahamdixon.com/archive/readArticle/296 (last accessed August 10,
2010).

the world seemed to these airy, joyful creatures. What did the bird know or see that we did not?

> What objects are the fountains
> Of thy happy strain?
> What fields, or waves, or mountains?
> What shapes of sky or plain?
> What love of thine own kind? what ignorance of pain?[15]

Shelley hoped that poetry might have visionary access to a higher and better world too. But music, freed mostly from words, is a distinctive form of access to an imagined tranquility, ignorant of pain. For the worrier, the right sort of music can meet fretfulness with its own uniquely harmonious alternative of order, expectation, and containment.

Music can always distract us from whatever we are doing because it can imaginatively take us somewhere else or allow us to be lost in rhythm, pitch, and form. Music can take a listener back to the first time a piece was heard or some other happily recalled moment. But music doesn't have to return us to any real place. Music doesn't have to be a kind of diary. And it doesn't always have merely to "distract." Music's peculiar power lies in its ability to open up inner worlds that exist through music alone, in the difficult-to-describe composite place of reason-and-emotion-and-something-beyond-both that music uniquely embodies. The working of complicated, well-crafted music allows imaginative access to a location where worry finds it hard to remain.

Contrapuntal music is, for me, the best antagonist to the fretful landscapes of worry. Sound counters the very essence, the form or

---

[15] *The Complete Poetical Works of Percy Bysshe Shelley* (Boston, MA: Houghton Mifflin, 1901), p. 382.

structure of worry, with an alternative, audible architecture. What contrapuntal music offers is direction and surety, harmony and order—exactly the opposite, if only for a while, of the tense troubles produced from *"what if . . .?"* Ancient philosophy thought the circling planets gave out sounds; that the music of the universe was an audible assurance of its overall harmony, of sense and purpose in the heart of things. There wasn't anything out of place there: no pain, no discord, no trouble. There was certainly no worry. The idea lingered in the nineteenth century as if the fantasy was hard to let go. When John W. Chadwick published the still-sung hymn, "Eternal Ruler of the ceaseless round | Of circling planets singing on their way"[16] in 1864, he was remodeling that ancient, pre-Christian idea that the nature of the universe could be expressed, and heard, as music. He was only one of many who thought about universal concord.

J. S. Bach, the best of all contrapuntal writers, offers a musical world informed by his Lutheran faith. His writing expresses a robust but perpetually graceful sense that there is order and purpose. Bach is sure that matters will work out. He has his own belief in the singing of the planets. His music can be sad and mournful, close even to the tragic. It is certainly not merely cheerful. Its reassurances go deeper than that and penetrate through minor keys, discords, and the expression of suffering into a world of heard security. Bach's writing never loses its rootedness in that which is designed. He never loses sight of the point to which he is moving. The center of Bach's aural universe is under control. Here's a portion from a fugue, the richest form of contrapuntal music, from the *Prelude and Fugue in a minor* for one of Bach's own instruments, the organ (BWV 543):

---

[16] *The English Hymnal with Tunes* (Oxford: Oxford University Press, 1906), Hymn 384.

Bach's music surprises with its invention; it never spurns the unexpected or the innovative. It's far from predictable. Yet at the same time, Bach composes in a way that reassures. Everything, whatever happens, fits. These lines of music grow out of the fugue subject (the main theme) and its counter-subject that have been heard at the beginning. And they combine in intricate ways, quietly dazzling. Their graceful combining is nowhere more impressive than in this moment above. The organ pedals (in the bottom stave) weave into the three upper parts, played on the keyboards. As the pedal enters with its version of the fugue subject, nothing disturbs the two upper parts: the new seemingly independent line becomes part of them, pursuing its own way yet also as part of something whole. And then, shortly afterward, the fugue subject enters again, two half-bars later, in the left hand. It neatly and expressively overlaps with what is already there, generating more harmonic progressions, a forward motion, a natural logic, a certainty that a journey is worth taking and that there is somewhere to go.

To say that Bach works like clockwork gives a wholly false impression. There's nothing mechanical and dull, rigid or predictable. There is, instead, flexibility and expression in the context of order.

Liberty and plan are made into sounds. With eloquence, there's rationale and destiny: a reassurance that, whatever happens, the future isn't to be frightened of.

Worry's born with reason. It's an intimate associate of any act of thought, of any assessment of choices that lie before us, any attempt to take control of our own lives and judge for ourselves. Reason makes morality possible and sense, decency, and judgment. Reason helps create human meanings; it creates the possibilities of rule by law, of discussion, of partnerships. But thought's gaunt companions are sorrow and insecurity, grief, and apprehension. Beside this distressing alliance of reason with pain, the expressive arts, visual and musical in particular, can answer a little, at their highest points, to the trouble that reason brought. Not for ever and not for long—but sometimes, for a while. The arts are not unreasoning and they can be reasoned about. But the knowledge they offer has the power to take the worrier for a moment somewhere else, outside reason, outside trepidation, while still in their own minds. These arts offer no mere "escape" from the world but an alternative, a counter. They're not valuable simply because they're an exit route but because of where the exit leads.

Such forms of creative expression are greater than the thought and skill that went into them and if the arts of music and visual form provide only fleeting visions, they also offer real moments of disclosure that can't be faked. Art can't offer a merely rational ground for hope. But it's hope, of a kind, which it promises all the same. Art comprises no "well-being" course; its *raison d'être* isn't therapy; it offers no education in how to *choose* happiness. It's the opposite of the self-help books, the profoundest rebuttal of HR's expectations, and the deepest alternative to the bland happiness of the modern West. The bequest of the arts, particularly of visual and aural forms, is a "vision" (seen or heard but always felt) of something which, for a moment, makes better and tougher and more grown-up sense. Such art alters, for a period, the nature of ordinary living. Music and the visual arts make commonplace existence less commonplace, a little more valuable, and on something like a higher plane because such aesthetic forms reach harmonies we seem to have lost altogether.

Art's blessings matter for many reasons. But they matter peculiarly to a worrier like me because art offers structures that are unlike, as nothing else is, the inside of my apprehensive, disordered, worrying mind.

And, for that, for a while—I give distracted thanks.

Acknowledgments

My gratitude to the following people who have helped me, in a variety of ways, to write this book though none is responsible for its errors or its views: Dinah Birch, Rachel Bowlby, Matthew Bullimore, David Cottrell, David Fairer, Stephen Farr, Stacey Glick, Alexandra Harris, Tilar Mazzeo, Katy Mullin, Stuart Murray, David Pipe, Stephen Platten, Stephanie Rains, Caroline Shenton, Mark Vernon, Marcus Walsh, and Jane Wright. A brief portion of my consideration of Woolf and Joyce derives from my essay on Modernism and worry listed in the bibliography.

Bibliography

[Anonymous], *Conquering Fear and Worry, Live Successfully! Book Number 3* (London: Odhams, c. 1938).

— *Don't Worry*, by the author of *A Country Parson* (New York: Caldwell, 1900?).

Arnold, Matthew, *Essays in Criticism* (London: Macmillan, 1865).

Attridge, Derek, *The Singularity of Literature* (London: Routledge, 2004).

Auden, W. H., *Collected Poems*, ed. Edward Mendelson (London: Faber, 2007).

Bell, Currer [Charlotte Brontë], *Villette* (London: Smith, Elder, 1889).

Bentall, Richard P., *Madness Explained: Psychosis and Human Nature*, new edn (London: Penguin, 2004).

Berne, Eric, *Games People Play: The Psychology of Human Relationships* (New York: Castle, 1964).

Braddon, Mary Elizabeth, *Lady Audley's Secret* (London: Tinsley, 1862).

Brown, Haydn, *Worry, and How to Avoid It* (London: Bowden, 1900).

Buckland, Ralph Kent, *Worry* (Boston, MA: Sherman, French, 1914).

Caramagno, Thomas C., *The Flight of the Mind: Virginia Woolf's Art and Manic-Depressive Illness* (Berkeley, CA: University of California Press, 1992).

Chwin, Stefan, *Death in Danzig*, trans. Philip Boehm (London: Vintage, 2006).

Colas, Emily, *Just Checking: Scenes from the Life of An Obsessive-Compulsive* (New York: Pocket Books, 1998).

Combe, George, *Elements of Phrenology*, 3rd edn (Edinburgh: Anderson, 1828).

Cuda, Anthony, "T.S. Eliot's Etherized Patient," *Twentieth-Century Literature*, 50 (2004), pp. 394–420.

Davis, Lennard J., *Obsession: A History* (Chicago, IL: University of Chicago Press, 2008).

Descartes, René, *A Discourse on Method*, trans. John Veitch (London: Dent, 1912).

Diagnostic and Statistical Manual of Mental Disorders, 5th edn (Washington, DC: American Psychiatric Association, 2013).

Ehrenreich, Barbara, *Smile or Die: How Positive Thinking Fooled America & the World* (London: Granta, 2009).

Eliot, George, *Daniel Deronda*, 4 vols (Edinburgh: Blackwood, 1876).

Eliot, T. S., *Collected Poems 1909–1962* (London: Faber, 1974).

— *Selected Prose of T.S. Eliot*, ed. Frank Kermode (London: Faber, 1975).

Empson, William, *Seven Types of Ambiguity* (London: Chatto & Windus, 1930).

English Hymnal with Tunes, The (Oxford: Oxford University Press, 1906).

Firestein, Stuart, *Ignorance: How It Drives Science* (Oxford: Oxford University Press, 2012).

Foulds, Adam, *The Quickening Maze* (London: Jonathan Cape, 2009).

Franzen, Jonathan, *The Corrections* (London: Fourth Estate, 2002).

Gilbert, L. Wolfe, *I Should Worry* (New York: Harry Von Tilzer Music Publishing, 1911).

Gissing, George, *New Grub Street* (Harmondsworth: Penguin, 1985).

Glasser, William M. D., *Choice Theory: A New Psychology of Personal Freedom* (New York: HarperCollins, 1999).

Gold, Matthew K., "The Expert Hand and the Obedient Heart: Dr. Vittoz, T.S. Eliot, and the Therapeutic Possibilities of *The Waste Land*," *Journal of Modern Literature*, 23 (2000), pp. 519–33.

Greenfield, Kent, *The Myth of Choice: Personal Responsibility in a World of Limits* (New Haven, CT: Yale University Press, 2011).

Guardian, The

Hardy, Thomas, *Far from the Madding Crowd* (London: Smith Elder, 1874).

Homer, *The Iliad*, trans. Samuel Butler (London: Longmans, 1898).

Hustvedt, Siri, *The Shaking Woman or a History of My Nerves* (New York: Henry Holt, 2009).

Irish Examiner, The

Iyengar, Sheena, *The Art of Choosing* (New York: Twelve, 2010).

Jerome, Jerome K., *Three Men in a Boat (To Say Nothing of the Dog)* (Bristol: Arrowsmith, 1889).

Joyce, James, *Ulysses: The Corrected Text*, Student edn, ed. Hans Walter Gabler with Wolfhard Steppe and Claus Melchior (Harmondsworth: Penguin, 1986).

Keedwell, Paul, *How Sadness Survived: The Evolutionary Basis of Depression* (Oxford: Radcliffe, 2008).

Kipling, Rudyard, *The Light That Failed* (London: Macmillan, 1891).

Kroll, Jennifer, "Mary Butts's 'Unrest Cure' for *The Waste Land*," *Twentieth-Century Literature*, 45 (1999), pp. 159–73.

Leader, Darian, *The New Black: Mourning, Melancholia and Depression* (2008, London: Penguin, 2009).

Leader, The

Leahy, Robert L., *The Worry Cure: Stop Worrying and Start Living* (London: Piaktus, 2005).

Lilwall, Clive, *How to Stop Your 67 Worse Worries* (Bloomington: Authorhouse, 2004).

Marden, Orison Sweet, *He Can who Thinks He Can, and Other Papers on Success in Life* (London: Rider, 1911).

— *The Conquest of Worry* (London: Rider, 1924).

Mill, John Stuart, *The Collected Works of John Stuart Mill*, ed. J. M. Robson, 33 vols (Toronto: University of Toronto Press, 1963–91).

Murray, Stuart, *Representing Autism: Culture, Narrative, Fascination* (Liverpool: Liverpool University Press, 2008).

Norris, Kathleen, *The Noonday Demon: A Modern Woman's Struggle with Soul-Weariness* (London: Lion, 2008).

O'Gorman, Francis, "Modernism, T.S. Eliot, and the 'Age of Worry,'" *Textual Practice*, 26 (2012), pp. 1001–19.

Orens, John Richard, "The First Rational Therapist: George Lincoln Walton and Mental Training," *Journal of Rational-Emotive Therapy*, 4 (1986), pp. 180–4.

Oxford English Dictionary, electronic edn, www.oed.com

Phillips, Adam, *Going Sane* (London: Hamish Hamilton, 2005).

Proust, Marcel, *Le côté de Guermantes* (Première partie), édition du texte, introduction, bibliographie par Elyane Dezon-Jones ([Paris]: Flammarion, 1987).

Rohrer, Glenn, ed., *Mental Health in Literature: Literary Lunacy and Lucidity* (Chicago: Lyceum, 2005).

Roth, Philip, *The Human Stain* (London: Vintage, 2005).

Rycroft, Charles, *Anxiety and Neurosis* (Harmondsworth: Penguin, 1968).

Sadler, William S., *Worry and Nervousness or The Science of Self-Mastery* (London: Cazenove, 1914).

Salecl, Renata, *Choice* (London: Profile, 2010).

Saleeby, C. W., *Worry the Disease of the Age* (Cambridge: Smith, 1907).

Sass, Louis A., *Madness and Modernism: Insanity in the Light of Modern Art, Literature, and Thought* (New York: Basic, 1992).

Scruton, Roger, *The Uses of Pessimism and the Danger of False Hope* (London: Atlantic, 2010).

Sebald, W. G., *The Rings of Saturn*, trans. Michael Hulse (London: Vintage, 2002).

Shakespeare, William, *The Oxford Shakespeare: The Complete Works*, 2nd edn, ed. Stanley Wells and Gary Taylor (Oxford: Oxford University Press, 2005).

Shelley, Percy Bysshe, *The Complete Poetical Works of Percy Bysshe Shelley* (Boston, MA: Houghton Mifflin, 1901).

Smiles, Samuel, *Collected Works*, 26 vols (London: Routledge, 1997).

Solomon, Andrew, *The Noonday Demon: An Anatomy of Depression* (London: Vintage, 2002).

Sontag, Susan, *On Photography* (London: Penguin, 1979).

Stephen, Leslie, *Sir Leslie Stephen's Mausoleum Book*, ed. Alan Bell (Oxford: Clarendon, 1977).

Thurschwell, Pamela, *Literature, Technology and Magical Thinking, 1880–1920* (Cambridge: Cambridge University Press, 2001).

Tighem, Patricia van, *The Bear's Embrace: A True Story of Surviving a Grizzly Bear Attack* (Vancouver: Greystone, 2000).

Trollope, Anthony, *Framley Parsonage* (London: Smith, Elder, 1861).

— *Orley Farm*, 2 vols (London: Chapman & Hall, 1862).

— *The Last Chronicle of Barset* (Harmondsworth: Penguin, 1986).

Trombley, Stephen, *All that Summer She was Mad: Virginia Woolf and her Doctors* (London: Junction, 1981).

Tugend, Alena, "Too many choices: A Problem that Can Paralyze," http://www.nytimes.com/2010/02/27/your-money/27shortcuts.html?_r=0 (last accessed February 4, 2014).

Tylor, E. B., *Primitive Culture: Researchesinto the Development of Mythology, Philosophy, Religion, Art, and Custom*, 2 vols (London: Murray, 1871).

Virgil, *The Aeneid*, trans. Cecil Day-Lewis (Oxford: Oxford University Press, 1986).

Walton, George Lincoln, *Why Worry?* (Philadelphia, PA: Lippincott, 1908).

Webster, Noah, *An American Dictionary of the English Language* (New York: Converse, 1830).

Wilson, Eric G., *Against Happiness: In Praise of Melancholy* (New York: Farrar, Straus and Giroux, 2008).

Wolpert, Lewis, *Malignant Sadness: The Anatomy of Depression* (London: Faber, 1999).

Woolf, Virginia, *Mrs Dalloway* (London: Vintage, 2004).

— *To the Lighthouse* (London: Vintage, 2004).

Worcester, Joseph E., *A Dictionary of the English Language* (Boston, MA: Hickling, Swan, and Brewer, 1860).

Index